The Observer's Pocket Series

GLASS

The Observer's Book of

GLASS

MARY AND GEOFFREY PAYTON

WITH 95 HALF-TONE
ILLUSTRATIONS AND EIGHT
PAGES OF COLOUR PLATES

BLOOMSBURY BOOKS
LONDON

PENGUIN BOOKS

Published by the Penguin Group
Penguin Books Ltd, 27 Wrights Lane, London W8 5TZ, England
Penguin Books USA Inc., 375 Hudson Street, New York, New York 10014, USA
Penguin Books Australia Ltd, Ringwood, Victoria, Australia
Penguin Books Canada Ltd, 10 Alcorn Avenue, Toronto, Ontario, Canada M4V 3B2
Penguin Books (NZ) Ltd, 182–190 Wairau Road, Auckland 10, New Zealand

Penguin Books Ltd, Registered Offices: Harmondsworth, Middlesex, England

First published by Frederick Warne & Co Ltd

This edition published by Bloomsbury Books, an imprint of
Godfrey Cave Associates, 42 Bloomsbury Street, London, WC1B 3QJ,
under licence from Penguin Books Limited, 1992

3 5 7 9 10 8 6 4 2

Copyright © 1976 Frederick Warne & Co Ltd

Printed and bound in Great Britain by
BPCC Hazells Ltd
Member of BPCC Ltd

ISBN 1-8547-1024-9

CONTENTS

LIST OF COLOUR PLATES

PREFACE

This book is intended for those who collect or are thinking of collecting glass; and equally for those who merely want to know more about the glass they see in museums, Stately Homes, salerooms and antique shops.

It is a vast field, and collectors tend to split up into cliques between whom there may be little communication—e.g. specialists in 18th-century drinking glasses; paperweights; clear coloured glass (such as Bristol blue or cranberry glass); opaque coloured glass (such as slag glass); scent bottles; sealed wine bottles; cameo glass; and many other such categories.

The development of the art of glassmaking has depended, to a very large degree, on the interchange of ideas between countries, often through the migration of craftsmen. An introductory outline has therefore been included covering the history of glass from the earliest times; so many techniques and styles of decoration still in use today were first perfected surprisingly long ago. The main part of the book, in alphabetical order, deals not only with British and Irish glass but with that of, for example, Venice, Bohemia, Germany and the United States, as well as with the main types of collectable items. For those whose interest has been aroused, appendices list books for further reading and museums that have notable collections of glass. There is an index to facilitate quick reference; this may be found particularly useful in looking up definitions of the sometimes baffling technical terms in which books on glass necessarily abound.

Difficulties in dating and attribution are far greater in glass than in pottery and porcelain, and most of the dates given in the book are of necessity only approximate. To those pausing on the brink of a fascinating hobby perhaps the best advice is to buy what you like the look of and not to worry too much about when and where it was made. Nevertheless, aids to recognition and warnings of pitfalls have been given where possible.

We are indebted to Peter Lazarus for his helpful comments and assistance in obtaining illustrations; also to Shirley Hartshorne for some of the photographs.

MARY PAYTON

GEOFFREY PAYTON

South Zeal

INTRODUCTION

Cross-references: Words in SMALL CAPITALS indicate references to main entries which appear in their appropriate alphabetical place.

One would not expect to be able to see through a mixture of sand and ashes, but that basically is what glass is. Nobody knows when first it was discovered that silica (e.g. sand) heated with an alkaline flux (a substance that assists fusion; e.g. soda) produced glass, but it seems a natural sequel to the Egyptian development, probably over 5000 years ago, of glassy glazes to render earthenware pots watertight. Either Egypt or Mesopotamia (i.e. Iraq) is usually regarded as the place of origin, although recent excavations have suggested that glass may have been made *c.* 3000 BC in western Asia (i.e. Turkey). Pliny, writing in AD 30, has a pretty story of Phoenician sailors in Syria, 2000 years before his day, putting their sandy-clay cooking pots in an extemporized oven of natron (soda) blocks taken from their cargo— and finding that they fused into glass.

The Egyptians had long been fond of beads, whether carved in precious stones or made of clay and coated in blue glaze; the next step was to make beads wholly of 'glaze', i.e. of translucent glass, and these have been found all over the Middle East. A turquoise blue was and long remained the favourite colour; from the greatest period in the history of Egyptian arts, the 18th Dynasty (1570–1370 BC), astonishingly lovely little blue glass vases have survived, some decorated with applied threads of white or amber glass. These were found in tombs at Thebes and are so finely made as to indicate a well-established tradition of beautiful and varied glassware. Such vases, some with handles and few over 4 in (10·2 cm) high, were chiefly used for cosmetics.

The link with ceramic glazes is again shown in the method of their manufacture. A solid clay mould of the desired shape was made; round this core, opaque coloured glass threads were coiled and fused by reheating; or possibly the core was dipped in molten glass; in either case the vase might be decorated with applied threads of glass in other colours, to form wavy or zigzag patterns. The clay of the mould was then removed by scraping (Plate 1). Some objects, e.g. the mask of a face, were made by kneading glass in its plastic state into a carved stone mould.

Alexandria, founded 331 BC, a cosmopolitan city dominated by Greek influences, became the centre of learning and the arts (including glass-making) during the **Hellenistic period** which lasted until Rome conquered Egypt in 27 BC. To this period belongs the use of opaque coloured glass in inlay, mosaic and millefiori techniques, and the first wheel-engraving and gilding.

The discovery of **glass-blowing**, by far the most important advance in glass history, was made at the end of this period; it is traditionally attributed to the Syrians, sometime after 50 BC. Syrian craftsmen, quickly copied by the Egyptians, learnt to blow glass into two-piece pottery moulds cut with complex patterns, using a fresh mould for each piece. Thus originated MOULD-BLOWN GLASS, the key to mass production of domestic hollow-ware as opposed to luxury glass; it led to a vast expansion of the glass industry throughout the Roman Empire. The Syrians also learnt to dispense with moulds, producing **free-blown glass.**

'**Roman glass**' is a term applied to wares made in most parts of the Empire in great quantity during the next four centuries, i.e. until the Sack of Rome (410) and the shift of power from Rome to Byzantium (Istanbul). Most of it was utilitarian—bottles, beakers, dishes, bowls—but there were also scent bottles, footed wine glasses with short stems, and other luxuries, and most of the decorative techniques we know had been mastered.

Alexandria probably made the clearest glass of antiquity and the industry flourished there until the 10th century; the Syrian tradition continued until the 15th century. Around AD 200 the use of manganese as a decolorizer was discovered; up to then most glass had been tinged blue or green by impurities in the sand used. The highlight of this era was CAMEO GLASS, e.g. well-cut portrait medallions and the PORTLAND VASE.

Of Byzantine glass little is known. The glory that was Greece passed from history, together with the grandeur that was Rome, and the stage was set for the Muslim conquests. By 750 Muslim rule extended from Spain through North Africa and the Middle East to India, though Byzantium itself held out until 1453.

During the **Islamic period** the traditional glass-making skills were preserved but the centres of activity moved gradually eastwards to Persia. Free-blown, mould-blown, wheel-cut and facet-cut glass was made. Damascus specialized in enamelled and gilded wares and revived trailed and ribbed decoration. Persian craftsmen excelled in highly elaborate and skilled undercut ('**caged**') glass and other engraving; they made attractive mould-blown green bottles with the characteristically Islamic tall slender necks. The best work, notably mosque lamps (fig. 1), dates from the 13th and 14th centuries. In 1402 Tamerlane swept all the Damascus craftsmen off to Samarkand, leaving the field clear for Venice to take the lead in every department of the development of glass.

Meanwhile, further north, skills learnt in Roman times were kept alive in the Rhine–Rhône–Seine region, mainly at Cologne. Typical were the 5th-century tall footless **cone-beakers** (fig. 2), in green glass decorated in the Syrian style with white threads. From them were developed the **claw-beakers**, with hollow claw-like protuberances applied all round the sides (fig. 3). Bottles, jugs and bowls were also made; all these have been found preserved in graves. The yellow or bluish-green tinted glass was made not with soda but with potash, obtained from wood-ash in the Rhineland (and hence called *Waldglas*, 'wood-land glass') or, further west, from burnt bracken (*verre-de-fougère*, 'bracken glass'). It remained tinged until decolorizing was reintroduced in the 16th century.

'Anglo-Saxon' beakers of this type found in England were probably imported. There is little evidence of any native glass-working until the Wealden glass-houses were established, the first near Chiddingfold, Surrey, *c.* 1226, by a Norman called Laurence the Glassmaker, using the resources of the ancient forest

1 (*above left*)
Mosque lamp,
Syrian, mid 14th
century (*Royal
Scottish Museum*)

2 (*above right*)
Cone-beaker,
green, *c* AD 475;
found in Bedfordshire
(*British Museum*)

3 (*below left*)
Claw-beaker, green
with blue trails,
5th–6th century;
found in Durham
(*British Museum*)

of Anderida for fuel and potash. In 1240 Laurence made clear and stained glass for Westminster Abbey (stained glass was a French speciality). The Wealden men also made free-blown and mould-blown *Waldglas* bottles and drinking vessels.

The medieval potash glass of Germany, France and England was crude peasant work; for a true revival of artistic craftsmanship Europe had to wait for Venice, where the industry dates from the 11th century and was perhaps advanced by the acquisition of foreign craftsmen when Byzantium fell to the so-called Crusaders (1202). Venice was by then an important seafaring state and a natural meeting place for Eastern and Western influences.

For fear of fire in the crowded city the glasshouses were moved, in 1291, to the neighbouring island of Murano, where they still are—some of the workers claiming direct descent from these early pioneers. Their island home made it easier to keep jealously guarded trade secrets, and savage laws were enacted to discourage emigration by those who knew them.

The Venetians used soda not potash as flux (see SODA GLASS), producing a brownish-yellow glass (*cristallo*; see VENETIAN GLASS) of notably light weight in which the characteristically graceful but fragile wares of Venice were made. No pre-1450 glass survives; the golden age of Venetian glass, when it was a luxury sought by all Europe, came in the 15th–16th centuries. Henry VIII imported some, at great expense; by Elizabeth's time much coloured Venetian glass was on sale in London. But in general it was too fragile to travel well, even by sea, or to last well; it was later to yield place to sturdier wares.

Venice did not succeed in keeping its formulae

secret. In addition to defectors from Venice, there was a long established industry at L'Altare near Genoa (Venice's bitterest trade rival), which was always happy to send its craftsmen anywhere for a fee; their products cannot be distinguished from the Venetian.

With the domination of southern Italy and of Spain by the Hapsburgs, there was a general shift of trade and wealth away from Italy via Spain to the Spanish Netherlands and elsewhere; the glass industry followed this trend. Thus the North Italian styles spread to North-West and Central Europe, which made its own versions of Venetian soda-glass wares (FAÇON-DE-VENISE) with the assistance of Italian glass-men (who reached Spanish-held Antwerp in 1541). Within a few years Antwerp ranked second only to Venice as a centre for fine glass. Spanish persecution then drove Huguenot craftsmen to England (it was from Antwerp that Jean Carré and Verzelini came to London), and within a mere half-century London replaced Antwerp as a glass centre and commercial capital. This spread of Venetian skills over Europe entailed severe competition for Venice itself and from 1700 there was a decline from which it did not recover until the mid 19th century.

In Elizabethan England the Venetian **Giacomo Verzelini** had become manager of a London glass-house established by Huguenot refugees. In 1575 he was granted a monopoly in the manufacture of Venetian-style soda glass, and the import of glass was prohibited for as long as he could make it at competitive prices. Only nine pieces of probable Verzelini work survive—all goblets, most engraved in diamond-point and dated.

Meanwhile it had been found that the old Wealden

glass industry (undoubtedly aided by the iron industry) was using up an enormous amount of timber from the Sussex forests, primarily required to build men-of-war. Surprising though it is that the requirements for glass should be significant, there are several references to it, and a similar problem arose regarding Bohemia's forests. There was even a petition that the glass-makers should be moved to Ireland to ruin the environment there instead! Window glass was the main product, and there was now a sudden demand for it to glaze the large country houses that were going up everywhere.

Elizabeth accordingly began to close down some Wealden glasshouses (1585) and James I (1615) banned altogether the use of timber for fuelling furnaces. Fortunately by this time a coal-burning furnace had been evolved (1611) and the glassmen were already moving nearer the coal (which they preferred to charcoal), first to Newnham near the abundant coal of the Forest of Dean, and then northwards—a process that established Stourbridge and Newcastle-on-Tyne as two of the chief centres. Most were still making *Waldglas*, particularly for bottles.

Verzelini's monopoly passed through less knowledge-able hands to reach Sir **Robert Mansell**, to whom James in 1618 gave absolute control of the whole industry, then employing some 4000 men, not only in the places mentioned but at King's Lynn (which had excellent sand), Swansea, Nottingham and as far afield as Fife (Wemyss). Transport of glass by wagon was hazardous; hence the centres were at ports (e.g. Bristol) or on navigable rivers.

In Mansell's time the typical old English wine bottle was introduced; earlier, bottles had been used for holy water, medicines and oils rather than wine. Mansell made both *façon-de-Venise* and cheaper tableware—e.g. beer glasses at half the price of their *cristallo* counterparts; he was the first to make mirrors on a commercial scale, using a Venetian technique. The Venetian ambassador in London admitted that Mansell's *cristallo* equalled Murano's in quality—but perhaps he wanted something. Mansell died in 1656 and the monopoly died with him.

At the Restoration (1660) an excessively unlikely figure surfaces briefly in the history of English glass—George Villiers, Duke of Buckingham, who, wrote Dryden, 'stiff in opinions, always in the wrong, / Was everything by starts and nothing long'. In between his various sojourns in the Tower of London he was allowed to enjoy the profits of a glasshouse in Vauxhall; nothing is known to have survived of its products, despite the name 'Vauxhall glass' optimistically bestowed on mirrors one cannot see one's face in.

From this immediately pre-Ravenscroft period date a few famous commemorative pieces in soda glass, e.g. the Venetian-style Royal Oak Goblet (see COMMEMORATIVE GLASS).

To turn to the Continent; the map of Europe has been so drastically redrawn that it is inappropriate today to use the term 'German' to cover glass made in Bohemia (now in Czechoslovakia) and Silesia (now in Poland and Czechoslovakia) as well as in the Rhineland or Nuremberg. But since German was the native language of much of this area (and of the rulers, for centuries, of most of the rest) the types of glass made have German names but are not necessarily of German origin. Similarly, 'Dutch' is used (incorrectly) of glass made in Flemish Antwerp, Walloon Liège and

Dutch Amsterdam alike.

While Italian craftsmen are said to have come early in the 16th century to Cologne, Nuremberg and Munich, there were many native shapes and decorative styles, still in potash *Waldglas*, that remained prevalent, indeed dominant, long after that time and owed nothing to Venice. *Waldglas* and Venetian *cristallo* thus overlapped. See GERMAN GLASS; BOHEMIAN GLASS.

ENAMEL PAINTING was very popular and is especially associated with Bohemia and Nuremberg from the 16th century onwards. Diamond-point ENGRAVING was perfected by the Dutch in the late 16th century, and to a lesser extent by Rhinelanders. Wheel-engraving, developed by Caspar Lehmann (*c.* 1600) and his pupil Georg Schwanhardt working at Nuremberg, became more elaborate later in the century. Johann Kunckel at Potsdam in the 17th century introduced a fine ruby glass by adding gold to the ingredients. In that century the new clear '**Bohemian crystal**' was introduced, heavy enough to stand up to the deep-cut engraving in which Bohemians and Silesians excelled.

In England, *c.* 1673, a decisive change took place when **George Ravenscroft** was appointed glass-maker to the Glass-Sellers Company of London. He had presumably read the translation (1662) of the Italian classic, Antonio Neri's *The Art of Glass* (1612) which had referred to '**glass of lead**' as 'known to few' and in colour 'the finest and noblest'; but, he added, it was far too brittle. At any rate, in 1675 Ravenscroft added a lead oxide to the new type of potash glass he had patented the previous year. The Venetians had already tried out red lead in some of their glass.

To begin with he probably tried using flints, but turned to lead because he found that they did not fuse easily. His glass is confusingly referred to as **flint glass,** but sand soon replaced flint and the qualities of the new English glass were due to lead, not flint. Various defects were gradually overcome (see LEAD GLASS), though possibly not until after Ravenscroft's death (1681). Some of his pieces are marked with a barely decipherable raven's-head glass seal; few survive, but they include bowls, posset-pots, ewers and what may be the first decanter.

The very nature of the new glass imposed a complete change from Venetian styles; thin walls and delicate applied ornament were not practicable. Instead there was simplicity and concentration on attractive shapes designed to display its striking qualities to best advantage. Light surface-engraving and, later, CUT GLASS were the preferred forms of decoration; heavy engraving, enamelling and intricate applied decoration were in general left to the Continentals. This policy paid, as English clear 'flint' glass was in great demand at home, and to some extent abroad, for the next 150 years.

To many collectors 18th-century English glass means, in effect, drinking glasses. It was indeed *the* century for these, but the detailed attention given them may perhaps have thrust undeservedly into the background many other categories, e.g. CANDLESTICKS, which were also at their best, besides many fine wares in coloured and OPAQUE WHITE GLASS.

In the first half of the century DRINKING GLASSES tended to be heavy and thick, plainly but well designed, with BALUSTER and SILESIAN STEMS predominant, and folded FEET; of these the Newcastle light balusters (1735) were an elegant and highly prized variation. TEARS, AIR TWISTS and OPAQUE TWISTS were introduced. Wine glasses in beautiful shades of blue and green were made, at Stourbridge and Bristol in particular, from about the 1760s onwards. Engraved JACOBITE GLASSES appeared in the 1740s, followed later by the WILLIAMITE. English engraving, with a few exceptions, was not notable until the late 18th century. By mid-century glasses were becoming smaller and lighter in weight. William BEILBY began enamel-painting clear glass at Newcastle and Michael Edkins enamelled opaque white at BRISTOL. COLOUR TWISTS came into vogue. English CUT-GLASS bowls, decanters etc. were an increasingly important feature, the cutting going deeper as the century progressed.

Excise duty on glass (see TAXATION) was imposed in 1745, more than doubled in 1777 and, together with the grant of Free Trade to Ireland (1780) which allowed the Irish to export to England for the first time for a century and thus widened the market available to them, led many English glass manufacturers to migrate to Ireland, where glass was still untaxed; thus began the heyday of IRISH GLASS or, more accurately, Anglo-Irish glass (1780–1850).

In 1793 NAILSEA (near Bristol) began making utilitarian wares of window-glass and then, increasingly, its brightly coloured frivolities or FRIGGERS. These were in fact made all over the country but the name 'Nailsea' was given them presumably because they made the first, the most or the best. The development throughout this and succeeding periods of DECANTERS and other BOTTLES, DESSERT GLASSWARE, CANDELABRA, FINGER-BOWLS etc. deserves more attention than it sometimes receives.

In general, 18th-century taste switched from the heavy ornate symmetries of Baroque to the more frivolous Rococo style (c. 1715) and a reaction (c. 1760) to the severer lines of the Neo-Classical style derived from the recent new discoveries of Graeco-Roman art; but the impact of all this on glass was less marked than in other fields such as furniture and ceramics.

On the Continent the preference for elaborate decoration continued. Nuremberg wheel-engraving tended to decline and to be surpassed in the 1720s by that of Bohemia and Silesia; typical examples are found on large-bowled covered goblets. Dutch engraving on English lead glass was also noteworthy; the Dutch had long excelled at stipple engraving, which became very popular for a time.

The newly invented German porcelain (1710) of Meissen (Dresden) and elsewhere made an impact on glass sales, and the Bohemian houses turned (as did Bristol) to making opaque white glass enamelled in imitation of it. A further threat to the European industry came later from the popularity abroad of English lead cut glass.

The first half of the 19th century was dominated on the Continent by Bohemian innovations in coloured glass, many due to the remarkable Friedrich Egermann (see BOHEMIAN GLASS). Much of this glass took the fancy of the Biedermeier period (1815–48), a nickname applied to products made for the stolid bourgeoisie of German-speaking lands. It also startled British glass manufacturers when they saw it displayed at the Great Exhibition (1851) and found that, possibly owing to taxation (not abolished until 1845), the home industry had fallen far behind Central Europe in exploring the new ways of exploiting glass which had been made possible by improved equipment and techniques.

French contributions of the period were OPALINE GLASS vases (1820s); PAPERWEIGHTS (1840s), some with SULPHIDES; and the ART NOUVEAU work of GALLÉ and LALIQUE at the century's end.

During the 19th century there was considerable interchange of ideas across the Atlantic. Two main regional centres had been established in 18th-century America—the first in New Jersey (1739), the second, by Stiegel (1769), at Manheim, Penn., supplying the Mid-West. These were followed by many more glasshouses, mostly in New England (see AMERICAN GLASS). In 1875 TIFFANY, in New York, turned his attention to Art Nouveau glass. The most far-reaching American innovation was PRESSED GLASS, invented c. 1825 and soon copied in England; this brought imitation cut glass within the reach of all. The 1880s saw an explosion of new types of coloured fancy glass, enumerated under COLOURED GLASS.

Britain in the 19th century continued such specialities as 'BRISTOL' BLUE and 'Nailsea'. In 1819 Apsley PELLATT (London) patented his sulphides. A quite different process produced the very expensive CAMEO GLASS (1847). Very fashionable in the 1880s, these are usually called Webb cameos, Webb of Stourbridge having engaged some of the best craftsmen to make them. Webb later also produced SATIN GLASS and the American BURMESE GLASS. Stourbridge had become a great centre for innovation, e.g. Richardson's opaline and frosted glass. Fairy LAMPS (1885) were also primarily a Stourbridge product, and SILVERED GLASS was made there. Whitefriars

(London) made (1860) ART GLASS in reaction against Victorian decorative excesses. Sowerby (Newcastle) made much coloured pressed SLAG GLASS and vaseline glass. In fact in the 1860–1900 period there was a bewildering variety of quite different types of glass, all in demand at the same time; this was supplemented by heavy imports of cheaper glass, especially novelties, and competition was fierce.

4 (*left*) AIR TWIST. Jacobite glass, drawn-trumpet bowl engraved with rose and buds; multiple-spiral air twist (*Sotheby's*)

5 (*right*) ALE GLASS. Ogee bowl engraved with rosebud spray; double-series opaque twist stem, conical foot (*Sotheby's*)

AN A–Z OF GLASS

Air twist (1740–65)   A group of peculiarly English drinking glasses with stems containing spirals of air. The commonest and earliest form is the multiple spiral of evenly spaced single air-threads (fig. 4); the names of the other kinds are fairly self-explanatory: the spiral gauze; corkscrew (single or double); mercury twist—a pair of thick corkscrews down the centre which reflect light in such a way that they look like mercury (this type was made of the very best glass); multi-ply spiral (bands of up to twelve gossamer-thin threads).   A single-series stem contains one form only; a double-series has one kind spiralling round another. See TEARS.

When it is added that some stems are knopped (these are highly valued), some glasses (possibly the earliest) are two-piece (i.e. stem and bowl in one piece; the majority are three-piece) and that air twists occur on most types of glass, it can be seen that the number of combinations could reach football pool proportions. In fact, the bulk of them are single-series multiple-spiral, either drawn trumpets (the commonest) or three-piece glasses, knopped or unknopped.   The most frequent double-series form has a central straight or twisted gauze surrounded by a pair of spirals.

The best examples have unbroken, evenly spaced threads.   The presence of folded or domed feet adds greatly to their value.

Ale glass   The English 18th-century ale glass usually

had a deeper narrower funnel bowl than the equivalent wine glass. Ales may be classified by stem length as standard (fig. 5), short and dwarf; there were also giant ales over 12 in (30·2 cm) high and what are sometimes called Georgian ales, both with larger capacities than the others. Dwarf ales may have no stem or only a knop separating bowl and foot. FLUTE GLASSES were also used for ale and champagne, and many of these types for cider (1740s), as is (rarely) indicated by an engraved apple tree or blossom, while ales are often engraved with barley designs, from the balustroid period onwards.

Unhopped ale (when hopped it was called beer and drunk from tumbler or tankard) was an extremely strong drink in the 17th and 18th centuries—hence the small bowls (by modern standards). It was very cloudy and to disguise the fact early ale glasses, especially dwarf ales, were wrythen, very deeply in 'Somerset ales', Somerset ale being the most alcoholic and presumably the cloudiest.

Amberina (1883) American glass, the first of the shaded-colour types of which BURMESE GLASS is the best-known. The shading effect, from fuchsia-red to yellow-amber, was produced by differential heating of glass to which metallic gold had been added (Plate 1). Most pieces are semi-translucent, but some are 'plated' with an opaque-white lining.

Another variety, **Agata**, was given a mottled finish by splashing Amberina with alcohol or other quickly evaporating liquid.

American glass The first name of historical interest is **Caspar Wistar** who, with workers from his native Germany, started a glassworks in New Jersey (1739–

6 AMERICAN GLASS. South Jersey-type sugar-bowl, bowl, jug, gimmel flask, sugar-bowl, mug; c. 1800–65 (*Corning Glass Museum*)

80); its reputation was due to its sturdy free-blown domestic wares in green or amber bottle-glass, some plain, some with applied decoration (notably the 'lily-pad'—i.e. water-lily leaf). Wares of this kind, made in many parts of Eastern USA until late 19th century, are given the generic name **South Jersey type** (fig. 6).

Another German-born American, **Henry Stiegel**, founded a glasshouse at Manheim, Pa. (1769–74), where workers from Germany, England and Ireland made 'flint glass' tablewares (i.e., probably, of fine quality soda-lime, not lead, glass) of great variety, including clear and coloured, moulded, engraved and enamelled (fig.7), in German or English styles. To Stiegel is attributed the **flip glass**, a moulded, fluted and engraved tumbler. Although so short-lived, the factory gave another generic name, **Stiegel type**, to similar wares made mainly in the Middle West. Few surviving pieces can safely be attributed to either

27

7 AMERICAN GLASS. Enamelled tumbler attributed to the Stiegel works, c. 1765–74 (*Corning Glass Museum*)

Wistar or Stiegel. A third generic name came from the Connecticut firm of Pitkin (1783–1830), whose ribbed pocket flasks in amber or green glass are now called **pitkins**. The most important early American glasshouse was that of J. F. **Amelung** in New Bremen, Md. (1785–96); again, founder and craftsmen were of German origin. They made tablewares, decanters etc. in a near-colourless non-lead glass, wheel-engraved in German styles; some pieces are signed and dated.

Fine lead glass was made from 1813, e.g. at Bakewell's of Pittsburgh (1808–82) which also produced cut glass and sulphides. Excellent Irish-style cut glass decanters and wines were also made by the New England Glass Co., Cambridge, Mass.

(1818–88), as well as cased glass, French-type paper-weights and **'blown-three-mould'**, i.e. mould-blown decanters etc. (see MOULD-BLOWN GLASS). The Boston & Sandwich Glass Works at Sandwich, Cape Cod (1825–88), founded by Deming Jarves specialized first in lead glass but soon became so prominent in the development of pressed glass that it came to be called **Sandwich glass**. Sandwich also made opaline (1830) and much cranberry and other coloured glass (1840s) as well as overlays. In this period (1815–70) there was a fashion for **historical flasks**, i.e. pocket whisky flasks moulded with portraits of celebrities and other commemorative (including electioneering) themes.

In the 1880s there was a search for coloured novelties, chiefly centred on Massachusetts. The New England Glass Co. made the first shaded-colour glass, AMBERINA and POMONA; the similar BURMESE GLASS was invented at another Jarves foundation, the Mount Washington firm of New Bedford. Other firms made KEWBLAS, PEACHBLOW and SPANGLE GLASS.

The largest modern glassworks, the Corning Glass Co. of Corning, NY, traces its descent from a Brooklyn firm (1823) and absorbed the Steuben Glass Works (1903–18) at Corning, which specialized in fancy glass, including the iridescent **Aurene**. Reorganized in 1933, Corning turned to high quality crystal glass, intaglio-cut to designs (some commemorative) by well-known artists such as Matisse and Epstein. See also MARY GREGORY GLASS; TIFFANY GLASS.

Art Deco (1920s–30s) A blanket term covering 'modernistic' styles evolved in the Jazz Age, partly in reaction to ART NOUVEAU, although many designers won fame in both styles.   Art Deco went in for massive shapes, strongly contrasted colours (e.g. black and white), crisp geometric designs and themes from nature (especially the sunburst); it also absorbed motifs from current discoveries, e.g. Tutankhamen's tomb (vases with Egyptian wing handles) and Aztec art (e.g. bowls).

The movement was dominated by Frenchmen, especially Maurice Marinot, the Daum brothers of Nancy and LALIQUE, whose aerodynamic radiator-cap mascots may be remembered (Plate 1; fig. 8).   See also PÂTE-DE-VERRE.   (French *art décoratif*, a term used in a Paris exhibition, 1925.)

8 ART DECO.
'Susane au bai
1925 (*Sotheby
Belgravia*)

9 ART GLASS.
Loetz vase, *c.* 1900
(*Sotheby's Belgravia*)

Art glass A vague term with at least two meanings.
(1) The products of individual artists who, in the
spirit of the Arts and Crafts Movement of the 1860s,
tried to restore artistic standards to an industry beset
by pressed glass and the Victorian taste for over-
decoration.   These included James Powell & Son at
Whitefriars, who specialized in hand-made pieces in
opalescent and pale-coloured glass; Louis Lobmeyr
(1890s) and his nephew Stefan Rath (*fl.* 1919–51)
working in Bohemia; the Bohemian firm of Loetz
(1900s; fig. 9); the French artists of ART NOUVEAU
and ART DECO; and TIFFANY.

(2) The various forms of fancy COLOURED GLASS,
much of it originating in the USA in the 1880s.
Stourbridge was the chief centre for English glass of
this kind.

Art Nouveau (1890–1910)   A *fin-de-siècle* style
evolved in reaction against the ugliness of the

Industrial Age, characterized by sinuous designs derived from plant life, especially the lotus and the lily, and a love of extravagant detail for its own sake. It drew inspiration through William Morris's Arts and Crafts Movement from Japanese motifs and the pre-Raphaelites. More prominent on the Continent than in England and taking its name from a Paris shop, L'Art nouveau (1895), its chief manifestations in glass were the work of GALLÉ, LALIQUE and TIFFANY.

Aventurine glass A glittering veined and spangled glass, dark reddish-brown flecked with gold, first made in 16th-century Venice by adding copper to the batch. It was discovered by chance (Italian *avventura*) when someone accidentally dropped copper filings into molten glass. That is the story; it seems more likely that it was aventurine, the variety of quartz which the glass resembles, that was discovered by chance and first so named.

Baluster and Balustroid (1685–1745) The baluster glass is the oldest type of English lead drinking glass. The 'baluster' is a short pillar, slender above, pear-shaped below (fig. 75), but this shape is less common than the inverted form, i.e. upside down, sometimes with a knop at the base, sometimes knopless. The name is rather misleading as it is used to cover glasses which instead of a baluster shape have prominent knop formations of various kinds (the mushroom is one of the most prized), and sometimes as many as five different knops on one stem (fig. 46). In most cases the glasses are very heavy and the bowl has a deep solid base, often containing a TEAR; tears are common in the stems also. Round funnel bowls and wide folded feet predominate.

Similar glasses, with lighter and usually taller stems, less heavily knopped and lacking (as a rule) solid bases to the bowl, are often separately classified as **Balustroids.** Their date is 1725–65 but in the latter part of this period many inferior glasses were made for the cheaper market, and these are usually the only balustroids seen today except in museums.

An interesting variation is the **Kit-Cat** with trumpet bowl and a plain stem over an inverted baluster. It is named after a painting showing members of the Whig Kit-Cat Club holding wine glasses of this kind (by their *feet*, incidentally).

Beaker A stemless vessel, in its earliest form (AD 100) conical, then cylindrical with a flared rim, with or without a foot-rim; from it the TUMBLER was developed. Early types are described in the Introduction, see figs 2 and 3. Beakers again became popular in 18th-century England, often engraved or enamelled (some by BEILBY). See fig. 95.

Beilby, William (worked 1762–78) The most famous of the English enamellers on glass, who worked at Newcastle with important assistance from Mary, his very young sister, and possibly from a brother, Ralph, who specialized in heraldic engraving. Some of their work is marked 'Beilby' but there has been the usual over-attribution of unmarked pieces to a famous name.

Genuine Beilby work, it is said, is characterized by designs entirely in a thick white enamel sometimes tinged (or perhaps discoloured by time) blue, occasionally pink, in a style resembling the 'Battersea' enamels of Bilston, where he had worked; and by (it is suggested) the inclusion in some designs of the dead branch of a tree or a butterfly as a kind of trademark.

33

His favourite medium for armorial decoration (fig. 36) was the bucket-bowled opaque-twist goblet, and his subjects included landscapes, ruins, sporting scenes, a little *chinoiserie*, fruiting vines, hops, 'exotic' birds (of the type common on porcelain; fig. 10) etc; also Masonic glass. Glass rims were usually gilded.

Bells Coloured glass bells, usually about a foot high, are a favourite type of FRIGGER with collectors. A very few were made in the 18th century but most survivors are mid 19th century, and even they frequently have the original clapper missing. The bells themselves were made in various colours (fig. 11) or opaque white, usually with Nailsea-type LATTICINIO decoration. The handles were even more varied and included ribbed, knopped and cut-glass types, others decorated with latticinio, colour twists or opaque twists, and a few in the shape of a hand or leg.

The earlier bells were in bottle-glass, possibly with reds and greens predominating; Victorian versions were in coloured (often blue) lead glass. But dating by colour is a doubtful exercise, and there are many modern reproductions, the best being French.

Bohemian glass The glass industry of the Kingdom of Bohemia (once ruled by the Hapsburgs of Vienna and now mostly in Czechoslovakia) was unique in that it was controlled by the aristocracy and sited mainly on their estates, especially in the mountain forests on the borders of Bavaria and Saxony. Early products resembled GERMAN GLASS, but from the 16th century Bohemia became and remained the home of many lasting innovations.

The arts of cold ENAMEL PAINTING and wheel

34

10 (*right*) BEILBY.
Wine painted with
'exotic birds'; opaque
twist stem (*Royal
Scottish Museum*)

11 (*left*) BELLS.
Blue and white bell
with clear handle;
first half of 19th
century (*City Art
Gallery, Bristol*)

ENGRAVING were acquired in the 16th century from the Venetians but transformed in style to suit Central European tastes. In the first half of the 17th century a new potash glass, rich in lime, was introduced (‘**Bohemian crystal**’). It was a great advance on its predecessors, clearer and stronger than Venetian *cristallo*, and when blown thick it could be carved like rock crystal. It was thus particularly suitable for the high-relief and intaglio wheel-engraving on thick-walled glass which was a speciality of 17th-century Bohemia-Silesia.

By 1700 the Bohemian heavy Baroque style had won wide recognition, the typical piece being the massive baluster-stemmed covered goblet with deep-cut designs and, later, additional engravings of biblical, allegorical, hunting, rural or heraldic themes and portraits of contemporary notabilities. They might be yet further ornamented with internal threads of ruby glass or aventurine. Besides goblets there were stemmed bowls, scent bottles and decanters decorated with the superabundant profusion of ornament appealing to the taste of the age. Some of the work requiring the highest skill was carried out in Silesia (part of the Bohemian kingdom until Frederick the Great conquered most of it in 1742), sometimes in the local purple-tinted Silesian glass (fig. 12).

In the early 18th century Bohemian craftsmen revived the art of ZWISCHENGOLDGLÄSER and later of enamel painting (fig. 13). Elaborate chandeliers were also made. Bohemian glassware was now being sold all over Europe and exported to America. In the face of growing competition from the new Meissen (1710) and other European porcelain, tableware in opaque white ‘milch’ glass was introduced (c. 1750),

12 (*right*)
BOHEMIAN GLASS.
Silesian goblet, early
18th century; wheel-
engraved with view of
London (*British
Museum*)

13 (*left*) BOHEMIAN
GLASS. Goblet
enamelled with
fighting horsemen in
the foreground;
c. 1740 (*British
Museum*)

37

painted in porcelain styles and undercutting porcelain prices; this is sometimes wrongly attributed to Bristol glasshouses (some of it was exported to England) which had begun to do the same thing for the same reasons.

By the end of the century Bohemia faced a certain amount of competition from a new quarter—English cut glass, and set about imitating it; a swing of taste away from Baroque ostentation to Neo-Classical simplicity swelled the demand for this, especially among the increasingly prosperous bourgeoisie. Once again Bohemia adapted itself to new conditions, but retained its traditional skill in, and taste for, engraving and enamelling. After the Napoleonic deluge had receded, skilled industrialists began to replace the landed aristocrats in control of the industry, often to its benefit.

There was now a change of fashion from clear to coloured glass. This was the era of the great innovator **Friedrich Egermann** who introduced or developed the jet-black HYALITH (1823); LITHYALIN (1828; a 'stone' glass); a less expensive form of ruby glass (see COLOURED GLASS); and various surface-STAINED GLASSES (1830), notably in gold and amber. Egermann's secrets were soon stolen for use elsewhere.

Other forms of glass made in Bohemia about this time include OPALINE; alabaster glass (pastel blue or pink, often gilded or silvered); fluorescent yellow (uranium) or green (copper) glass, usually cut and gilded, a vogue of the 1830s and 1840s; SULPHIDES; and above all OVERLAYS, first developed commercially in Bohemia, together with the cheaper flashed glass.

Engraving was still the dominant ornamentation,

e.g. on goblets decorated with portraits or views of cities, castles or countryside—popular for sale to tourists, especially at fashionable spas such as Carlsbad.

The era of cheap pressed glass then set in but led to a vigorous reaction towards ART GLASS about the end of the century, led by Loetz and Lobmeyr. Another late 19th-century introduction was the so-called MARY GREGORY GLASS.

Boots and shoes   A remarkable range of boots (high-heeled cowboy-style, buttoned, and jack-boots), shoes (with buckles) and slippers were made in glass from the early 17th century. They were traditionally regarded as luck-tokens (sometimes used to decorate wedding-cakes). Many are supposed to represent a derisory punning reference to Lord Bute, Britain's worst prime minister, execrated as a bad landlord.

This type of toy is found in vaseline, Bristol blue, slag, spatter, opaque white and overlay glass. Most are miniatures but some were large enough to be used as flower vases, stirrup-cups and, allegedly, for drinking the toast 'Down the Bute', or even as a trick glass presenting the same hazards as the YARD-OF-ALE.

Bottles   Glass bottles have been made since Roman times and usually from crude unrefined materials; hence the prevailing green or amber colour of bottle-glass. Their efficiency, which depends on the toughness of the glass, was not great until annealing was improved in the 1720s. They were at first of an elongated egg shape and had to lie on their sides.

The earliest flat-based bottles in England seem to have been of the shaft-and-globe shape made (in glazed pottery) from *c.* 1630; only in 1690, after the development of lead glass, were bottles made in quantity of glass. From the earliest times all bottles had a high kick in the base to keep the rough pontil mark off the table, and a string-ring below the neck mouth, round which a string was tied to keep the cork in. Later the cork (a 15th-century invention) was pushed right in, as today, and the ring moved up to the top of the neck as mere ornament.

The early round-bodied bottles (fig. 14) became, in the 1740s, less bulbous and finally achieved straight sides, either with a squat wide-diameter body or with the tall, narrow, cylindrical body and long neck usual in wine bottles today. Both shapes were made from this time onwards; the latter was more convenient for binning, i.e. storage on its side in order to keep the cork moist and airtight, a practice more prevalent after port came into favour in the 1730s.

14 BOTTLES.
Onion-shaped; seal comprises Queen's head, 'R.W.' and '1690', for The King's Head Tavern, Oxford (*Sotheby's*)

The **sealed bottle** is the type that interests collectors; applied to the body of the bottle was a pad of glass impressed with the name, initials or crest of a supplier, tavern, private owner or university college, and sometimes the date. The earliest intact example is dated 1657, and they continued in use, at any rate in the colleges, until c. 1850; special sealed bottles were even made to commemorate Queen Victoria's Jubilees. Most college bottles come from Oxford, few from sober Cambridge, except from Emmanuel. There are rare sealed bottles with handles, e.g. one dated 1717, differentiated as *serving-bottles*, probably used until the true decanter ousted them.

Tall **Dutch gin bottles** with square bases and very short necks were made from the 17th century; later examples, some marked 'Geneva' (i.e. 'gin'), had the sides tapering down to a smaller base. Other square-based bottles were made to fit into travelling cases.

Old patent **medicine bottles** are now collected, of every kind and shape—especially valuable if still labelled or in sinister blue (indicating poison); a few are dateable to the 17th century. Collectors like the Odol tooth-paste bottle in milk glass because it ceased to be made in a known year, 1895.

Mineral-water bottles, made from c. 1800, are now finding a place in museums and attracting collectors, rather surprisingly. One of the earliest was the **Hamilton** egg-shaped bottle (1814), stored horizontally to keep the cork moist. The ginger-pop bottle, with a glass marble held tight against the bottom of the neck by the pressure of the gas, was sold with a separate wooden cap designed to press the marble down with a satisfying pop; it was often embossed until c. 1910, then labelled. Invented (1872) by Hiram

Codd of Camberwell, it was used till the 1930s; his name unexpectedly survives in the term 'codswallop', i.e. Codd's inferior beer (gingerbeer). In the 1870s the screw stopper was invented, and a stopper held in place by a swivelled metal device which was pushed aside to open. The crown 'cork' and bottle-opener followed in 1892. See also BRISTOL BLUE; FLASKS; SCENT BOTTLES; TABLE GLASS.

Bowl-shapes In dating 18th-century English drinking glasses the shape of the bowl is a poor guide, although it is possible to give a rough indication of the periods when some of them came particularly into vogue. From the beginning of the century perhaps the commonest forms were the round funnel, bell (fig. 52) and bucket; the ovoid, trumpet and conical (or straight funnel) were also fairly common from the early decades onwards. The round funnel (fig. 63), popular in the preceding century, remained so throughout the 18th century, becoming wider and shallower in later years. It is sometimes found in a pan-topped or double ogee form (fig. 26), which may be lipped; but this shape is more typical on sweetmeats. The thistle was an early development from the bell. Mid-century favourites included the ogee (fig. 5), sometimes with a flared rim, the waisted bucket and the two-piece drawn trumpet (fig. 87). From c. 1770 'Georgian' wines and ales (which had larger capacities) came into fashion. Other shapes are mentioned under ALE GLASS, CHAMPAGNE, CORDIAL, DRAM, FLUTE GLASS, RUMMER.

Bristol The first Bristol glasshouse was founded in 1651 by one of the Italian Dagnia family which started the Newcastle glass industry. At first the main output was bottles for the local wine trade. By 1696 Bristol was second only to London in the number of its glasshouses and during the next 150 years or so the industry flourished; but by 1874 Bristol was down to a single glasshouse.

Although clear glass (now unidentifiable) predominated in the total production, Bristol's reputation was won by its opaque white, BRISTOL BLUE and other coloured glass (fig. 35). Because of this reputation much glass made in these media elsewhere has since been attributed to Bristol. The only truly authenticated Bristol wares are the relatively few that are marked, but deductions can be made from these regarding the distinguishing features of true Bristol. Far too little is known, however, to make 'Bristol' more than an antiques trade name in most cases.

The most famous of the glasshouses was founded by **Lazarus Jacobs** (not later than 1775). He died in 1796 but his son, Isaac, carried on until at least 1806. They gilded and sometimes enamelled Bristol blue wares, a few of which, including decanters, wine-glass coolers (fig. 93) and finger bowls, are marked 'I. Jacobs Bristol' and dated; they also for a few years employed **Michael Edkins**, who had worked for other Bristol firms (1760–87). Edkins (died 1811) is thought to have specialized in decorating opaque white; but his fame was inflated by the attribution to him (corrected *c.* 1925) of Beilby's work at Newcastle. Bristol 18th-century opaque white looks like porcelain; having a high lead and tin-oxide content it was expensive and is now rare. Some white tea-caddies (fig. 66), vases and scent bottles (figs 78 and 79) are attributed, with no great certainty, to Bristol. Because the enamelling of much white glass resembles that on the 'Battersea'

43

enamels made at Bilston (near Wolverhampton), it is now usually more safely classified as 'South Staffordshire'.

Many green decanters possibly made in Bristol and embellished with floral decoration, as well as blue decanters gilded with exotic birds, may have been decorated at the **James Giles studio** in London (1760–78), more famous for work on porcelain (Plate 2).

After blue, green is the most eagerly collected colour (fig. 15). Green scent bottles and sets of labelled decanters and bottles resembling those described under BRISTOL BLUE are generally accepted as Bristol. Between the wars, reproductions in both colours were made in England and Czechoslovakia. See also neighbouring NAILSEA.

Bristol blue Lead glass of a distinctive and extremely attractive deep blue, with a purplish tint where thick, sea-blue where thin, made with a colouring agent imported through Bristol. Hence, and hence only, its name, for 'Bristol' blue was made in many other parts of England.

15 BRISTOL. Group of green wines (*Harvey's Museum*)

The colour was due to the addition of a particular form of cobalt oxide (zaffre) which was obtained from Dresden by the William Cookworthy who later pioneered English hard-paste porcelain at Plymouth and Bristol. (Zaffre, incidentally, was the source of the pigment cobalt-blue, much used on porcelain.)

Its import (c. 1761–93) was interrupted by the Napoleonic wars, and England had to turn to native (Cornish) cobalt, which gave a harsher tint, and then (1804) to artificial aquamarine which had no purple in it and varied from greenish to reddish blue according to composition. Import was resumed c. 1820 and a fine 'King's blue' was made until 1840, when demand waned. Some say that true Bristol blue has an oily feel.

The best-known wares are the sets of (three or four) tapered decanters and of smaller condiment bottles, in stands. These were gilded with an imitation of the more usual silver chain and label naming the contents— e.g. 'rum', 'shrub' (a currant-juice and rum concoc-tion), 'hollands' (gin) on the decanters (Plate 2); 'ketchup', 'soy', 'essence of lemon', 'anchovy' on the bottles. The initial of the name was also gilded on the stopper, which was sometimes facet-cut. Next in present-day availability come finger bowls and the similar WINE-GLASS COOLERS; a gilt Greek-key frieze round the rim is thought to be typical of Bristol. A few of the decanters and bowls are marked—see BRISTOL. Scent bottles, toilet-water bottles, vases (Plate 2) and patch-boxes are also found in Bristol blue.

Burmese glass (1885) An almost opaque SATIN GLASS, shading from salmon pink at the top to pale yellow below; attractive only when illuminated and

16 CAGED GLASS. The Lycurgus Cup, Roman, 4th century AD; Lycurgus, King of Thrace, who unwisely provoked Dionysus, is being choked to death by a vine. The openwork is attached to the main wall only by minute bridges left in the under-cutting (*British Museum*)

hence much used in Fairy LAMPS and, as an occasional *tour-de-force*, in chandeliers and candelabra. Some pieces have gilt or enamel decoration and many have frilled edges and foot-rims (Plate 3).

Invented at the Mount Washington Glass Co., New Bedford, Mass., who sold some to Queen Victoria, it also had a brief vogue in Britain when made under licence (1886) by Webb of Stourbridge (marked 'Queen's Burmese'). It was expensive to make, gold producing the pink and uranium the yellow.

Caged glass A development from CAMEO GLASS which entailed exceptionally skilled and patient undercutting of the design so that it is almost detached from the body of the vessel. Some remarkable bowls and cups so decorated (e.g. the Lycurgus Cup; fig. 16)

46

date from the 4th century and are thought to be Syrian. There are also Islamic examples.

Calcedonio   Coloured glass imitating veined stones, especially onyx and agate and other varieties of chalcedony, made in Venice from the 15th century, and in England and Bohemia in the 19th century. It is now called *Schmelzglas* ('enamel glass'), a term which also includes AVENTURINE GLASS.

Cameo glass   Cased glass (see OVERLAY) relief-cut to produce much the same effect as a cameo cut in stone; usually the outer casing, which takes the design, is opaque white and the inner lining, which forms the background, is often blue (in this resembling the Wedgwood pottery cameo), though it may be in various shades of green, yellow or red, or there may be three layers (e.g. white, blue, red). The cutting is a difficult and laborious task, yet it was mastered in Roman times at Alexandria, notably in the PORTLAND VASE (AD 100).

Interest in this almost lost art was revived in 1876 when John Northwood of Stourbridge completed an exact replica of the Portland Vase. He passed on his skill to his son John (1870–1960) and to George and Thomas Woodall, who were employed by Thomas Webb of Stourbridge, a firm which produced so much cameo glass (fig. 32) that '**Webb cameo**' has become a generic term covering that made by other Stourbridge firms; some pieces are dated and marked, e.g. 'Woodall' or 'Webb's Gem Cameo', and the presence of a butterfly in the design is thought to be another Webb trademark (Plate 3).

A rough outline of the design was first obtained by removing unwanted glass with acid; this was then carved in detail and might be finished with wheel-engraving. Years might be spent on one piece and the price would be accordingly high. English designs tended to pander to the late Victorian taste for Classical figures in flowing drapery (fig. 17); more attractive are those showing Moorish or Japanese inspiration, many featuring a profusion of flowers, foliage or fruit. Vases, scent bottles and bowls are the chief forms, and the Woodalls' pre-Raphaelite plaques fetch high prices. Much sought are those carved on the type of quilted SATIN GLASS known as mother-of-pearl.

Standards had declined and the vogue had waned by the end of the century. Specimens most commonly seen today have thin casings etched through entirely by acid; the bottom was reached with imitations in which the glass was simply painted in very thick enamel.

17 CAMEO GLASS vase (*City Art Gallery, Bristol*)

French cameos were very different in style, avoiding the stolid Stourbridge obsession with fussy detail. The leading exponent, Émile GALLÉ, first exhibited examples in 1889; he influenced the Daum Brothers of Nancy, who produced floral designs and even landscapes in cameo.

Candelabrum A branched candlestick for the table to take up to four candles (later more usually two); one type has a central candle-holder higher than the others. The earliest known English example in glass (1695) has four short branches on a knopped stem, standing on a domed terraced foot. The branches were welded into a single unit which fitted into a deep socket in the main stem. The general style, e.g. of sockets and pendant drops, followed that of the CANDLESTICK, but there was scope for additional ornament such as festoons of linked drops between the branches, delicate spires of glass surmounting the stem and also hung about with pendants, and serpentine arms between the candle-branches carrying pendants only. Later, ormolu and other metal fitments were sometimes used, and bases of Wedgwood jasperware. There are many Continental reproductions.

The **wall-light** or **sconce** for fixing to a wall or over a mirror was of similar construction; some of them so elaborate that they look like halves of a chandelier.

Candlesticks Early glass candlesticks, from Venetian times onwards, copied silver shapes, and in England this tradition continued to some extent to Regency times when a Neo-Classical version on a fluted column and square terraced foot appeared. But the majority of 18th-century candlesticks followed the fashions of other glassware, e.g. stems might be Silesian, air twist, opaque twist etc; cut-glass examples came in with the 1740s and became progressively more elaborate; opaque white specimens appeared in the 1750s, painted with floral designs. As candles left to burn too low cracked the glass, loose replaceable nozzles were fitted from c. 1720.

Nearer the end of the century the fashion for pendant drops was established; the flanges under the candle sockets were widened to carry a circle of drops which (as with CANDELABRA and CHANDELIERS) were successively pear-shaped, elongated 'icicles' (like pendant ear-drops) and finally sharp-edged prisms up to 6 in (15 cm) long. After the turn of the century these might be arranged in two tiers and completely hide the candlestick—a development that led later to the LUSTRE VASE. The term **girandole-candlestick** for these is perhaps best avoided; 'girandole' had many meanings in France (where it now means 'chandelier') and after its adoption in England was given several more (including 'candelabrum').

Among numerous variations were the use of coloured glass for the stick or the drops; bases of jasperware mounted in ormolu; stems in the form of a dolphin (a Victorian fancy); and many designs in pressed glass. Towards 1900 cut glass fell out of favour and glass candlesticks were no longer made.

Tapersticks (c. 1690) were shorter, much slenderer affairs to hold candles of only pencil thickness (fig. 18). They were probably used at the writing-desk to melt sealing-wax; or, with scented tapers, at the tea-table; and possibly as an all-purpose source to light tapers, pipes etc. from before matches came in (1830). Some

18 CANDLESTICKS.
Taperstick,
c. 1730–50 (*Royal
Scottish Museum*)

of them are most attractive, with knops, twists or cut decoration, and they have therefore been reproduced in modern times. **Chamber-candlesticks** of glass were made in the early 19th century but are very rare.

Early candles might be of expensive scented beeswax or of common tallow; the latter guttered badly and needed constant trimming. An improved wax candle appeared about 1740, giving more light and less trouble; the greatly improved paraffin wax candle that we know today had to await the discovery of petroleum (1859), but by that time gas was becoming the common domestic illuminant.

Old glass candlesticks are often very attractive,

whether in plain graceful metal-ware shapes or in the later more elaborate glittering versions.

Carafe Basically a stopperless decanter, used from the 18th century to serve wine or water at table, and called **water-craft** or table water-bottle. It may be difficult to distinguish one from a decanter which has lost its stopper unless a frosted neck gives it away. Carafes in general followed decanter styles and might be cut, engraved or left plain. Later the name was down-graded to refer to the squat version, with matching tumbler, found on Victorian wash-hand-stands; later still, to the plain restaurant vessel.

Carnival glass (1880s) American coloured pressed glass given an iridescent sheen in imitation of some Tiffany glass. Mass produced for fairings etc., much of it in an unattractive marigold but some in purple, green etc., it was made into all kinds of tableware, including breakfast sets, and even a decanter with matching wine glasses, though plates and dishes are commonest. Carnival glass is classified by patterns, in many of which grapes are present; other motifs are windmills, peacocks, kittens and butterflies, but there are countless others.

Champagne White and red varieties of still wine from the Champagne district and called 'champaign' first reached England in Charles II's reign (1660), and were drunk from FLUTE GLASSES, since they carried much sediment. Another type of glass was intro-duced from Hanover c.1705; they had very wide-rimmed ogee bowls, often on Silesian stems, and may have been used both for champagne and as sweetmeats (see DESSERT GLASS; fig. 19), though the latter more

19 CHAMPAGNE. Champagne glass (or possibly a sweetmeat) on Silesian stem (*Christie's*)

usually had scalloped edges or an everted rim which would have made them impossible to drink from.

Sparkling champagne did not overtake the still variety in popularity until *c.* 1760. The modern shape of champagne glass came into fashion *c.* 1830.

Chandeliers The earliest chandeliers were used to light churches and were of metal; in the 16th century Venice made them of natural rock crystal. The glass chandeliers used in the state rooms of palaces and large houses appeared in the 17th century both in Venice and in England; since they were in effect candelabra suspended from a ceiling, their successive styles resembled those of CANDELABRA, although of course larger and more lavishly rococo in design. The earliest English survivor dates from *c.* 1740 and has twelve branches but no pendant drops. As with

the humbler candlestick, the main shaft in Regency times was often completely hidden by cascades of drops, sometimes in tiers (see CANDLESTICKS). Even in the most luxurious homes, these elaborate affairs were only lit for state occasions.

Gas chandeliers appeared in the 19th century, and were sometimes later converted to take electric light. Chandeliers that have survived from early years have commonly had extensive repairs and replacements, or are made up of odd but genuine bits and pieces. Imported Continental reproductions abound.

Claret jug Basically, a tall, slender, ewer-shaped decanter with a handle, a pouring lip and a decanter-style stopper or silver-mounted lid. Made from Ravenscroft days, comparatively few of the elegant Georgian examples have survived; but in the 19th century claret jugs, including (from mid century) coloured ones, were common enough (fig. 20).

Coin glasses   Small silver coins were occasionally enclosed in the knops of drinking glasses even in Venetian times.   English glasses (usually balusters) with Stuart coins are probably JACOBITE and those with post-1688 coins WILLIAMITE.   Coins were (and still are) also inserted to commemorate coronations or purely for decoration (fig. 60).   Tumblers, tankards and jugs may have coins in the base.   The date of the coin does not of course date the glass.

Coloured glass   In this context the adjective means *intentionally* coloured, as opposed to early glass coloured by impurities.   The ancients preferred their glass coloured; not until Venetian times was there any great urge to achieve colourlessness.   But Venice was even more famous for coloured glass, much of which was imported into England as, later, were quantities of coloured BOHEMIAN GLASS.   Yet on the whole clear glass was much preferred in England until mid 19th century, even though, in addition to BRISTOL BLUE, a wide range of English decanters, drinking glasses (including air and opaque twists), jugs, bowls etc. was made throughout the 18th and early 19th centuries in beautiful shades of green (see BRISTOL), amethyst, ruby and pale blue—much of it from Stourbridge.   Purple glass survives from an even earlier date.

Ruby glass was made by Johann Kunckel in Potsdam (1679) by an expensive and difficult process involving the use of gold and three firings.   The colour resembled red ink; it was closely imitated in Birmingham about a century later, and other ruby tints were obtained afterwards with selenium instead of gold. In Bohemia in the 1820s Egermann was able to make much cheaper ruby glass with copper, and this was often used in overlays; also rosaline (rose-pink).

A lighter, transparent cherry-red, usually called **cranberry,** was widely made in Victorian days and later—both in England and America—especially jugs, vases, wines, sugar bowls. Much of it was decorated with threads and frills of pinched clear glass (or tinted green or yellow); the better Victorian wine glasses have a collar between stem and bowl, and a domed foot—features lacking in later versions, which may also be pinker because they were blown thinner. A deeper tawnier red appeared in Edwardian times.

The extensive importation of coloured glass (including OVERLAYS) into England in the second quarter of the 19th century revived interest in all varieties among British glass manufacturers. The most popular colours were still green and blue. From the 1880s there was a spate of new types of fancy glass (originating mainly in America), e.g. CARNIVAL, AMBERINA, BURMESE, PEACHBLOW, SATIN, SPANGLE, SPATTER, SLAG and ART GLASS of various kinds. See also NAILSEA GLASS; OPAQUE WHITE GLASS.

The chief sources of colour are: for *blue,* cobalt (reddish), copper (turquoise); for *green,* copper, iron, chromium, uranium; for *red,* gold, copper; for *yellow*, silver, antimony. Manganese produces various shades of amethyst, violet or purple. Colours were varied by temperature and other conditions, by the metal used (lead or soda), and by combinations of colouring agents.

Colour twists (1750–80) A category of glasses

with a stem usually in mixed form, nearly all of them combinations of colour twist and opaque twist, combinations with air twists being very rare. The best colours are of opaque enamel glass, which shows to greatest advantage in combination with opaque white; translucent colours by themselves are usually too pale to be attractive. Sometimes the opaque white is edged with colour. Canary is the most sought-after colour, followed by green and purple; there are also blues, rubies, blacks, pinks and tartans.

Colour twists are very rare and very attractive (Plate 4); therefore the buyer must beware, e.g. of modern Continental reproductions in rather garish colours; danger signs are twists that seem too far below the surface, unsymmetrical or discontinuous. Ill-proportioned soda glasses with bell bowls and one or two colours plus opaque white are of contemporary Dutch manufacture, and said to have an oily feel.

Commemorative glass The Romans had glass commemorating chariot races; the Venetians similarly recorded gondola races. In the 16th century the Low Countries went in for marriage and betrothal glasses; later, notable Dutch examples were engraved by Jacob Sang on English glass (c. 1750–60). See figs 39 and 63.

A famous English example is the Royal Oak goblet made for Charles II's marriage (1663); also the Exeter tall flute (which may however be Dutch) of about the same date, engraved with the king's portrait and a stricken oak. Apart from the JACOBITE and WILLIAMITE GLASSES, there are those engraved with the White Horse of Hanover (1750), and portraits of Frederick the Great. Among the rarest are the

Privateer glasses, some of which came from Bristol, the chief port from which the privateers sallied forth to harass French shipping (1750s). The many Volunteer regiments have glasses engraved in their honour (1760s on) and the Sunderland Bridge (1796) was a great favourite on northern rummers (fig. 31). Most of these were wheel-engraved. See also MASONIC GLASS.

Royal subjects included the coronations of George II (drinking glasses), George III (mugs), William IV (Apsley Pellatt scent bottles). Brierley Crystal made scent bottles, goblets, flasks and mugs on the occasion of the Silver and Diamond Jubilees, the coronations of Edward VII and George VI etc.

During the 18th century many pieces were made for societies, trade associations ('Success to Trade and Navigation'), craft guilds or for sporting events. There also 'Friendship' glasses, some Dutch-engraved and more naive ones gilded by Absolon of Yarmouth; one popular glass is inscribed 'May the Wings of Friendship Never Loose a Fether'. Goblets, tankards and firing glasses were used and, particularly in the 19th century, rummers commemorating Nelson, Wellington, Earl Howe etc. See also TUMBLERS.

The coming of pressed glass permitted cheap mass production, e.g. amber dishes and candlesticks for the 1887 Jubilee and jugs showing newly launched ships, portraits of celebrities etc.

Composite stem (1740–60) A small group of glasses whose stems comprise two main types, the commoner being a multiple-spiral air twist over a plain section joined by a knop. Far less common is the opaque twist plus plain stem; other combinations are rare. Made of the best lead glass, probably at Newcastle, for the luxury market, they are today hard to find and expensive.

Cordial The cordial glass had a tiny 1 oz bowl on a tall very thick stem, most commonly on knopless air or opaque twists (fig. 21). Cordials developed in the 1730s from the oddly named 'semi-cordials', which had stems of normal proportions.

21 *(left)* CORDIAL. Cordial glass with floral engraving; double-series opaque twist, conical foot (*Sotheby's*)

22 *(right)* CORDIAL. Ratafia glass, round funnel engraved bowl, single-series opaque twist, folded conical foot (*Sotheby's*)

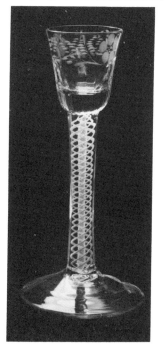
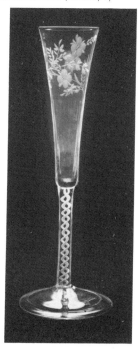

First mentioned in 1663, cordials were the English liqueurs, brandy-based, very potent, sweet and flavoured with fruit juices or peel, or with herbs. Reputed to be heart stimulants (hence the name), their real 18th-century purpose was to counteract the effects of too much tea after too much dinner. So cordials, served from small decanters, were drunk by ladies in the withdrawing room after dessert, while the men got down to the port.

The bowls, small as they were, are quite often engraved, e.g. with Jacobite emblems, vines etc.

A distinctive cordial drink, **ratafia** (*c.* 1700), was a cherry brandy flavoured with the kernels of almonds or peaches, and with cherry and apricot. It was drunk from a special glass with an exceptionally narrow tall tapering flute bowl on a stem of the same height (fig. 22). Some think these were used for other cordials, e.g the well-named **surfeit-water** (1750s), said to be twice as potent and to contain 80% brandy. See also TOASTMASTER'S GLASS.

Crackle glass   A form of glass, also called **ice glass**, first made in 16th-century Venice and revived in mould-blown form in the 19th century. It was given a cracked ice appearance by one of two methods: dipping the half-blown vessel in cold water, or rolling it in fragments of glass of a different composition, thus producing artificial crazing.

Crystal glass   A colourless, highly transparent glass of high refractive index, frequently used for tableware (British Standards definition). The term is reserved for glass of good quality and derives from *cristallo* (see VENETIAN GLASS).

23 CUT GLASS. Sweetmeat with shallow slicing and simple faceting, *c.* 1735 (*Royal Scottish Museum*)

Cut glass The product of a form of wheel-engraving chiefly associated with English and Irish lead glass, to which it added such brilliance. Faceted patterns were evolved that gave optimum light-collecting and reflecting properties and could be ground on the wheel relatively quickly. Thus various diamond patterns and stars became the commonest, as fulfilling both criteria, but curved motifs were more difficult.

The wheels used for wheel-engraving proper (see ENGRAVING) were small and (primarily) of copper; those for cut glass were larger and made of iron (to rough out the pattern initially), sandstone (to smooth the cuts) and of various other materials (to polish and to give a final finish to details). As with other wheel-engraving, the actual grinding was done not by the wheel but by liquid abrasives fed on to it. The term 'cut glass' is reserved for hand-cut glass, which in general is sharper edged, better polished and more brilliant than its imitations in MOULD-BLOWN and PRESSED GLASS; it also has the slight irregularities of pattern always associated with handicraft.

It is unlikely that English glass was cut before 1735, though possible that earlier pieces (e.g. sweetmeats) were given cut decoration at a later date. The scalloping of rims and feet was one of the earliest forms, and the cutting of drinking-glass stems with diamond or hexagonal facets (see FACETED STEM). Cutting was shallow at first (fig. 23) and did not become really deep until after methods of annealing (toughening) glass, already improved c. 1740, were further improved some forty years later, and until the foot treadle for turning the wheel was replaced by mechanical power. The brilliance of cut glass was further enhanced after the turn of the century when improved furnaces came into use.

TAXATION was another factor; deep cutting required thick walls—almost twice as thick, sometimes, as the finished product—and tax had to be paid even on the glass removed in cutting. It was taxation, too, that gave Ireland its opportunity (see IRISH GLASS; figs 50 and 83–86); hence the belief that the deep-cut glass so fashionable in the 1790–1830 period was mostly Irish. In fact, a great deal of it was made in England, but necessarily for the luxury trade; nevertheless, it found a ready market, so it seems that it was regarded as better than the Irish, which was considerably cheaper.

Popular in the Anglo-Irish period was a diamond-patterned band between double grooves; also horizontal prismatic step cutting, e.g. round the shoulders of decanters (this is associated with Bristol). Diamond patterns of growing complexity included the popular strawberry diamond (relief diamond with a flat top itself engraved with 16 small diamonds in relief) and the hobnail (the flat portion incised with a star); much used also were 'blazes' of parallel grooves, vertical or slanting. Other common motifs were stars under the base (1805), printies (circular or oval pits; 1820s), sprigs (or arrowheads) and vertical flutes rising from the base. On very slender evidence, curved motifs are attributed to Waterford, the vesica cut (a large pointed oval usually enclosing a star) and sunburst (a printie with radiating cuts) to Cork.

English cut glass was much admired abroad and several Continental firms (e.g. in France) started to make lead glass and to cut it in the English style. Ironically enough, by the time the English tax was lifted (1845) cheaply produced pressed glass was pricing cut glass out of the market and it was moreover going temporarily out of fashion, possibly under the influence of Ruskin's remark (1853) that all cut glass was barbarous.

Production did not however cease, and some Anglo-Irish products of the last half of the century were good enough to pass for late Georgian (and do so). During the inter-war years much cut glass was imported from Czechoslovakia and elsewhere and there was a large-scale home production of 'early Irish' candlesticks, sconces, chandeliers etc., some of them of deceptively good quality. Some reproductions are moulded and the principal and more accessible facets are polished up on the wheel; the less accessible facets give them away. Another point to watch out for is the grinding out of chips.

Cut glass is again in favour; much is made at Water-ford, by Webb of Stourbridge and Edinburgh, and by Stevens & Williams of Brierley Hill near Stourbridge.

Decanters These appeared in the Ravenscroft period, and gradually superseded the serving-BOTTLE. Transitional forms include a clear-glass version of the shaft-and-globe bottle; a six or eight-sided mallet shape, also with a long neck; and the curious cruci-form decanter, with the body deeply scalloped into a cruciform shape (in section) so that the iced water in which it was stood could most efficiently cool the wine. These early decanters resembled early bottles in having a string ring (for the cork; there was no stopper) and a kick; few have survived.

The early stoppered decanters had shorter necks and the body might slope outwards to a fat base (fig. 24) or taper inwards from the shoulder like an Indian club; the pontil mark and kick disappeared *c.* 1750. In the Anglo-Irish period (1780–1850; see IRISH GLASS) the most popular shapes were the cylindrical (with sloping (fig. 25) or horizontal shoulders) and the Prussian, a slender barrel-shaped decanter, often with three neck-rings. There was a great variety of neck-ring arrangements on Regency and later decan-ters, three being the usual number; they were intended to aid the grip, but were gradually discarded in the 1860s. Short-necked square decanters were also made from early in the century, originally to fit into travelling cases, eventually to appear in the Victorian lockable tantalus for spirits. The **ship's decanter** (1780s) or **Rodney** (named after the admiral) sloped out to a very wide base, for stability in rough seas.

Until *c.* 1745 stoppers were not ground and there-

24 (*right*)
DECANTERS. English,
wheel-engraved
'Claret' etc., 1760
(*Royal Scottish
Museum*)

25 (*left*)
DECANTERS. Marked
'Penrose Waterford',
c. 1795 (*National
Museum of Ireland*)

fore not airtight. Shapes, in order of appearance, were: hollow ball; spire finial; vertical disc, including the bull's-eye or target form; pear-shaped (associated with Bristol blue); and the mushroom, typical of the 19th century. Stoppers are often replacements; it is important that they should match the decanter in style and hue of metal, besides fitting well.

After *c.* 1755 there might be an engraved imitation of the silver label and chain naming the contents, e.g. ale, cider, champagne, mountain (Malaga wine from mountain grapes), shrub, Lisbon; sometimes vines or hops were engraved on the other side. Later, labels might be gilt or, occasionally, in white enamel.

Cut decoration, often displayed at its best on decanters, followed the styles described under CUT GLASS, culminating in the over-decorated mid-Victorian type derisively dubbed 'cut-and-slash'. Coloured decanters became popular *c.*1780 (see BRISTOL BLUE; COLOURED GLASS) and OVERLAY examples in the following century. There was a popular revival of Georgian shapes and styles from the 1920s onwards. Some extremely clever 20th-century forgeries, with 'Cork Glass Company' impressed on the base, have been made in England or Holland.

Depression glass Cheap American pressed glass tableware in amber, blue, pink etc., made by many firms during the Depression that followed the Wall Street crash (1929).

Dessert glassware An early Georgian dessert was virtually a separate stand-up after-dinner party—an occasion for the ostentatious display of silver, porcelain

26 DESSERT GLASSWARE. Sweetmeat, Silesian stem, double ogee bowl, domed folded foot (*Christie's*)

and glass; but by the end of the 18th century dessert had dwindled into the last course of dinner.

Two main categories of dessert would be on offer: **dry sweetmeats**, eaten with the fingers, e.g. preserved fruit, nuts, raisins; and **wet sweetmeats,** eaten with a spoon, e.g. trifles, rich spiced custards, hot fruit jellies. There could also be fresh fruit, cheese, chocolates, dried orange chips and spiced wines. Several of these had their special glass vessels.

The dry sweetmeat glasses (figs 19 and 23) were in general more decorative and typically had a wide double-ogee bowl on a tall Silesian light baluster stem, the rim of the bowl being usually lipped (fig. 26); others had flared rims, turned-over serrated edges or rims surmounted by tiers of openwork loops. Cut-glass decoration was fashionable from the 1770s. Many glasses had fairly small shallow bowls on tall stems which followed the fashion of the day—air or opaque twist etc. Others again might have wide shallow (*tazza*-shaped) bowls on a short stem.

In addition there might be small **comfit glasses** on rudimentary stems, primarily for comfits (tiny sugared breath-sweeteners—yesterday's chlorophyll); **compôtes** or **preserve jars**, covered stemmed bowls for preserves, pickles etc. (good mould-blown specimens were still being made in the early 19th century); and **ice-cream glasses**, thick-walled wide-brimmed conical glasses on rudimentary stems.

Some of these would be arranged on pyramids of up to four glass **salvers** (or **tazze**) of diminishing size—stemmed flat dishes on wide domed feet, usually galleried (fig. 27); or in elaborate glass

27 DESSERT GLASSWARE. Salver with jelly glasses and a 'captain' glass (*Laing Art Gallery*)

épergnes (Plate 4), bowls on stems into which were socketed candelabrum-style branches from which hung little glass baskets and perhaps lustres. Dining-table **centre-pieces** of this kind were made in coloured glass for a revived late 19th-century vogue, e.g. in ruby glass with hanging baskets for fruit or nuts.

Wet sweetmeat glasses typically have fairly deep capacious bowls on a short stem at first, later rudimentary. The foot developed from the folded and domed to square, and back to rounded form by 1800. Most were left plain, but others had fluting, serrated or scalloped rims or, occasionally, light engraving.

Attempts have been made to differentiate between **jelly** and **custard glasses**, but the general consensus now seems to be that although they appear in many different shapes, they were used indifferently for either purpose, from *c.* 1715. Others think a wide-loop handle rising higher than the brim is the mark of the jelly glass. At first they had twin handles (sometimes double-looped) and a thick-walled deep waisted trumpet bowl. Later there was a single handle or none (fig. 27); the walls became thinner; the bowl might be a deep bell, conical or double ogee; and the glass became taller and larger. In the 19th century there were many cranberry 'custards' with clear handles; and also debased specimens used in shops to sell ices in.

Dram (1710s) A squat glass to hold up to 3 oz. (85 ml) of spirits; it was either very short stemmed or stemless. Most drams had terraced feet, some thick and solid (see FIRING GLASS); the commonest form had a trumpet bowl on a plain stem; some were

28 DRAM. Sham dram, opaque twist, terraced foot (*John A. Brooks, Rothley*)

engraved with Jacobite or Masonic emblems. Glasses with ovoid bowls and thin ('oversewn') or thick ('overstrung') glass threads radiating from the base of the stem to the rim of the foot are found from the 1770s; also cheap pub drams.

Sham drams or **deceptive drams** (1810s) had the same semi-solid bowls as the TOASTMASTER'S GLASS and for much the same reason, to spare the abstemious landlord when plied with drinks (fig. 28). Later ones may be in other shapes (e.g. stemmed bucket-bowl) and have folded feet although made in the 19th century of inferior metal.

A curiosity is the **double dram**, in which the foot is replaced by another bowl, of different size and shape, joined by a plain stem; these were probably used as measures.

70

Drawn stem   A two-piece (**straw-shank**) glass in which the stem is not made separately but is drawn from the bowl; it is found in association with nearly all the facet stems, and also with many plain straight stems and some air twists.   See figs 4 and 87.

Drinking glasses   English 18th-century glasses are classified by their STEMS; they are also differentiated by BOWL-SHAPE, FOOT and KNOPS, features less useful in dating a glass.   Glasses may be two-piece (**drawn or straw-shank**), with the stem drawn from the bowl, or three piece (**stuck-shank**), in which bowl, stem and foot are separately fashioned and then welded together.

Specific types include Ale, Beaker, Champagne, Cordial, Dram, Firing, Flute, Goblet, Mead, Punch, Rummer, Syllabub, Toast-master, Toasting, Toddy-rummer, Tumbler (see entries under these headings). It is uncertain which types of glass were used for claret and port.

After c. 1725 glasses showed a general tendency to become smaller, lighter and no longer plain, but decorated with TEARS, twists, applied decoration, colour (blue and green), cutting, engraving or, more rarely, enamelling.

In buying old glass there are many points to watch. The edge of the bowl-rim and of the foot should be rounded and smooth; if it feels flat or sharp it has probably been trimmed to eliminate a chip.   A trimmed or chipped bowl-rim is anathema to the collector, but a foot in this condition may be acceptable if the glass is sufficiently rare or interesting.

Old clear lead glass should have a smoky (bluish-green or greyish) tint, best seen against dead-white paper, and especially by looking at the bowl base or down on to its rim; modern glass is very white, and fakes often have a coppery tinge. Differentiation between lead and soda glass is dealt with under SODA GLASS.

The pincers that held the glass while the pontil rod was severed leave vertical marks that can just be seen if the glass is turned slowly in the light; and there may be slight **striations** round the inside of the bowl, or on the foot, resembling the sand ripples left by a receding tide. The underside of the foot should show signs of wear where it touches the table; these scratches must be entirely random—faked wear usually betrays itself by parallel marks, rubbed too deep.

There exist many very clever English and Dutch reproductions of early glasses, especially balusters, air twists and opaque twists. If in lead glass, the darkish tinge may be missing; soda glass should be easily detectable. There may be slight imperfections in twist stems. (Many of these points are taken, with permission, from an unpublished paper, No. 127, read to the Glass Circle.)

Early Victorian drinking glasses were often in cut glass or, after 1845, in a wide range of colours; a little later the fashion was for coloured bowls on clear stems and feet, or for clear bowls lightly engraved with an overall pattern of small stars, ferns or a machine-produced Greek key design round the rim. Bowls became very thin-walled, stems very slender. See also COMMEMORATIVE GLASS; RUDIMENTARY STEMS.

Dumps The usual name for solid flat-based egg-shaped pieces of green window-glass used as door-stops (weighing up to 6 lb; 2·7 kg) or, if only egg-sized, as paperweights. They were associated with Nailsea in the early 19th century, and later with the North Country glasshouses.

The typical dump is pale green and encloses a bubble design of silvery sprays of flowers and leaves covered with dewdrops (fig. 29). This effect was achieved by the simple but ingenious process of rolling hot glass over a design chalked on the marver (a metal table), and casing it with another layer of glass, which caused the chalk to oxidize and form gas bubbles. An earlier method was to form a fountain of pear-shaped bubbles by lancing the hot glass core with a metal pin, creating cavities over which the cooling glass congealed.

29 DUMPS. Green bottle-glass door-stop enclosing floral motif; late 19th century. Height 4 in (13·2 cm) (*City Art Gallery, Bristol*)

Rare variations are made of smoky lead-glass, or contain coloured glass flowers, animal figures or millefiori designs.

Dutch and Belgian glass *Façon-de-Venise* glass was made at Antwerp, Liège and elsewhere in the Low Countries from *c.* 1550 to 1700, when English-style drinking glasses (but in soda, not lead glass) came into fashion. ROEMERS were also made from an early date. But the main Dutch contribution to antique glass was in ENGRAVING, both diamond-point and wheel (figs 33 and 39).

Enamel glass An older term for (mainly German) OPAQUE WHITE GLASS, misleading on three counts: it fails to mention either of the significant characteristics; some of it was not enamel-painted but transfer-printed; and enamel painting is used on clear, coloured opaque and opaque white glass alike.

Enamel painting For permanence, mixtures of pigments (including white) from metallic oxides together with a flux, technically known as **enamel colours**, had to be fired on to the glass (as on porcelain) at fairly low temperatures. Colours simply painted on and left unfired ('cold painting') soon wore away in use. The technique was known from Egyptian times and was used on clear and coloured glass.

The best, most brilliant and elaborate examples came from Bohemia (fig. 13) and Germany (figs 42 and 43) in the 16th–18th centuries; much Bohemian work was until recently wrongly attributed to Nuremberg. Armorials predominated, but portraits, religious themes, hunting scenes, conversation pieces, scenery

74

etc. are common. Outstanding work was done in black by Johann Schaper at Nuremberg (1660s). Early examples were all painted in opaque colours; transparent colours were first used by the Mohns of Dresden (fig. 30) and Vienna (1800s), followed by Anton Kothgasser, also in Vienna, who decorated tumblers with a wide variety of subjects, usually signing his work.

In England enamelling was less important and is chiefly associated with two names in the 1760s–80s: William BEILBY of Newcastle, working in white enamel (fig. 36), and Michael Edkins of Bristol painting on opaque white glass (fig. 66); but far more is attributed to them than they could possibly have performed. There was a revival at Stourbridge in mid 19th century, using vivid colouring and gilding on both clear and coloured glass in a wide range of designs. See also MARY GREGORY GLASS.

30 ENAMEL PAINTING. Mohn tumbler, depicting Dresden; 1790–1812 (*Cinzano Collection*)

English and Scottish glasshouses Some of the
main centres of historical (and in some cases con-
tinuing) importance are mentioned below, together
with their more distinctive products.

Alloa. From 1750 made many Nailsea-type
friggers and bottles.

Birmingham. George Bacchus & Co. made the
first English overlays (1851), many paperweights, and
opaline glass. Rice Harris at the Islington Glass
Works also made paperweights.

Bristol. See BRISTOL; BRISTOL BLUE; NAILSEA.

Edinburgh and Leith. Leith became the chief
Scottish centre in the 18th century. Friggers were
made there, and a firm founded in 1864, later moved
south of Edinburgh, became famous for 'Edinburgh

crystal' tableware, now made for Webb (see Stour-bridge).

London. James Powell & Son became prominent *c.* 1875 at Whitefriars and in 1922 the Whitefriars Glassworks moved to Wealdstone, Middlesex. One of the family was a leader in the Arts and Crafts Movement and was responsible for excellent 'Anglo-Venetian' pieces (1880–1904). Specialities included paperweights, silvered glass and opaline glass. See also Apsley PELLATT.

Newcastle upon Tyne. An important centre in the 18th century (see NEWCASTLE DRINKING GLASSES; William BEILBY). Thereafter glass manufacturers tended to move to Gateshead and Sunderland (fig. 31). At Gateshead, Sowerby (now Sowerby Ellison Glass

32 ENGLISH AND SCOTTISH GLASS-HOUSES. Cameo vase on light green ground; marked 'Thomas Webb & Sons' (*Godden of Worthing Ltd*)

Works Ltd.) was famous for all kinds of coloured pressed glass, e.g. slag glass ('vitro porcelain'), and for opaline glass, marked with a peacock's head.

Perth. John Moncrieff Ltd. and its predecessors from the 1860s made artistic ('Monart') tableware in blended colours. Paul Ysart's modern paperweights made first at Perth, later in Caithness, are of high quality.

Stourbridge was famous for coloured glass even in mid 18th century and a hundred years later had taken over the leadership in glassmaking from London. Thomas Webb & Sons (1837) pioneered cameo (fig. 32), Burmese and other art glass and still makes fine crystal tableware. W. H. B. & J. Richardson made much pressed glass, overlays, cameo, frosted and two-colour opaline glass. Stevens & Williams of the Brierley Hill Glass Works (1776) have made (Royal) Brierley Crystal since the 1890s. They also made cameo and silvered glass.

Engraving There are three main types of engraving on glass: diamond-point (including stippling), wheel-engraving (surface and deep) and acid etching. CUT GLASS is a form of wheel-engraving but is treated as a separate category.

In **diamond-point engraving**, practised even in Roman times, narrow opaque lines are scratched with a diamond or a steel stylus. The Venetians revived this art in mid 16th century, but the fragility of their glass caused difficulties and decoration was chiefly confined to border rim patterns.

Naturalistic precision on curved surfaces is difficult to attain by this method; this did not suit the Germans, and supremacy in diamond-point was left from the 16th century to the Dutch (figs 39 and 63). They used cross-hatching of varying density to obtain light-and-shade effects (*chiaroscuro*). These effects were vastly improved by the use of stippling, either alone or in combination with line engraving. In this method, which became almost a Dutch monopoly, tiny dots are gently tapped into the glass, traditionally with a hammer. Laurence WHISTLER taps by hand alone and doubts whether early engravers used a hammer; hammering would seem to be not only infinitely tedious but hazardous, especially on soda glass. The intensity of highlights depends on the closeness of the dots, the plain surface representing shadows and background. The results are amazing, sometimes reminding one of spiritualist photographs of ectoplasm except that the picture is rendered in great detail. A gifted amateuse, Anna Visscher, and her sister seem to have introduced stippling (c. 1610) and it was developed in the 18th century by Frans Greenwood (fig. 33) and David Wolff among others, often on English lead glass, especially Newcastle light balusters.

England did not excel in any form of engraving. Apart from the rather formal work on Verzelini goblets (c. 1580) and such exceptional pieces as the Exeter flute, which may well have been Dutch-engraved (see COMMEMORATIVE GLASS), English diamond-point began c. 1720, featuring at first armorials, arabesques and scrolls. Most of it is commemorative (fig. 51) or presentation glass, particularly (after mid century) rummers with hunting, coaching and rural scenes. These are also found in Victorian times, together with designs in trailing leaves, ferns (1850s–70s) and tiny stars (1880s).

In **wheel-engraving**, a difficult art also practised

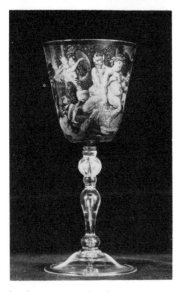

by the Romans, the glass is cut by holding it against one of a series of wheels revolved rapidly by treadle and fed by hopper with an abrasive mixture; it is the abrasive, not the wheel, that does the cutting, leaving a greyish mark on the glass. The technique derives from gem cutting. Varying effects are produced by varying the wheel's size, material (usually copper but also stone, cork or rubber), and the degree of polishing (with a wheel of lead or wood). Wheel-engraving gives a coarser line than the fine hard line of diamond-point.

This technique, again, was not suitable for Venetian glass. The traditional 'father' of the type called **surface engraving** to distinguish it from the later low and high relief engraving, was Caspar Lehmann, the Emperor's lapidarist, who seems to have worked in Prague, Nuremberg and Dresden; his only signed work is dated 1605. He founded the 'school' of Nuremberg engravers, notably Georg Schwanhardt (*fl.* 1640–60s) and his son Heinrich. The first to combine wheel and diamond-point on one glass, they specialized in tiny landscapes surrounded by scrolls, usually on the tall covered Nuremberg goblet—an elaborate affair with numerous knops and collars. Heinrich also engraved **calligraphic glasses** with mottoes in florid lettering surrounded by scroll-work. The Nuremberg tradition spread to Frankfurt-on-Main, Dresden, Potsdam and elsewhere, the main themes being armorial, commemorative and landscape.

By 1720 Bohemia had surpassed Nuremberg and the German states in this kind of work, especially pictorial (fig. 12) and armorial designs. The Dutch, notably Jacob Sang (*fl.* 1752–1800) also executed very fine surface engraving, often on the relatively soft English lead glass, e.g. landscapes and shipping scenes remarkable for their perspective effects.

The distinctive contribution of Bohemia and Silesia, from *c.* 1690, was in two deeper forms of wheel-engraving: **low relief** (*intaglio, Tiefschnitt*), akin to gem cutting and intermediate between surface engraving and the sculptural **high relief** (*Hochschnitt*), which was akin to cameo carving. They were rendered possible by the invention of 'Bohemian crystal' (see BOHEMIAN GLASS), in which heavy-walled goblets and beakers could be carved like rock crystal. Low-relief 'carving' produced deep wide lines which were partially polished; the method imposed restriction to formal designs, e.g. foliage, scrolls, strapwork, and the abandonment of landscapes and portraits.

The chief early practitioners (of both forms) were a Silesian family—the brothers Winter, one working in

Silesia (1687), the other in Potsdam, and their nephew Gottfried Spiller, also at Potsdam, who surpassed them. But the greatest exponent of the laborious high-relief technique (though he did both), in which the design was undercut and stood out sharply, was their contemporary, Franz Gondelach of Cassel.

From 1750 interest in wheel-engraving declined, to be revived in Bohemia c. 1825, especially on OVERLAYS. In the 19th century Bohemia produced fine surface engravings, particularly on ornamental goblets; the best were portraits, but there were also views of castles, hunting and rural scenes and religious themes.

English wheel-engraving dates from c. 1730 and was at first confined to rim border designs. Technically and artistically inferior to Continental work, it nevertheless included interesting categories of commemorative (fig. 31) and Masonic glass (fig. 60), portraits (fig. 89) and numerous designs of vines and grapes or hops and barley. In many cases old glasses have been used for quite recently added engraving (especially Jacobite); this can sometimes be detected by the greater whiteness of the cuts; another sign may be blunted edges instead of firm outlines, caused by trying to speed up the work by etching.

In **etching** the design is bitten out by hydrofluoric acid; this can be done in two ways. A thin 'resist' of wax was engraved through to the glass with a steel point and the acid applied; or, in a reverse process ('acid embossing'), the background was etched away with a tool dipped in acid, leaving the design standing out in relief. Etching gives a thin pitted shallow line; it is less expensive but less effective than other methods. In England it was not taken up until the

82

1830s; in 1857 Benjamin Richardson patented a commercial process for use on coloured tableware.

Faceted stem (1770-1810)   A small group, almost all two-piece wines, made of the best metal for the luxury market but until recently relatively cheap. Only one in five of the 18th-century glasses had knops (shoulder or central).   Bowls are usually ovoid or round-funnel, often engraved (many by Dutch engravers), the later ones with standard Regency motifs or armorials.   Of the unknopped glasses about half have diamond facets cut on the stem (fig. 34) and most of the rest, hexagons; the feet are sometimes also cut to match.   After 1780 most facet-stem glasses were made in Ireland.

Moulded-facet stems were made in the 19th century and still are.   Vertical fluting and scale cuts, formerly very rare, became common and there was a great variety of facet-cut knops.

34   FACETED STEM.
(*Prestons Ltd,
Bolton*)

Façon-de-Venise Glass which closely imitates the early Venetian styles, primarily that made in Holland, Germany and England during the 16th and 17th centuries. After the revival of the Venetian glass industry in the 1830s there was a corresponding revival of *façon-de-Venise* elsewhere, e.g. English examples in these styles at the 1851 Exhibition, *vitro di trina* and other forms of LATTICINIO being favourites. In addition much Italian *façon-de-Venise* was (and still is) imported into England, that made by Antonio Salviati (Plate 5) in the late 19th century being of high quality.

Fakes, forgeries and reproductions Strictly, while **forgeries** are 100% fraudulent, the much commoner **fake** begins life as a genuine piece but has had 'Value Added', e.g. engraving; a **reproduction** is a copy possibly made with honest intent but turned into a fake, e.g. by removing the star mark that makes a Gallé piece post-1904; a **replica** is an exact copy. In practice these terms tend to get mixed up.

There are few features of old glass that cannot be, and have not been, skilfully faked or reproduced. Of genuine old glass bogusly engraved the commonest are Jacobite air twists, Amen, Williamite and Privateer glasses. 'Irish' cut-glass is another favourite. German or Bohemian enamelled glasses, including roemers, have been copied with great care, French paperweights less carefully. Colour twists, cameo glass, Nailsea wares and even the yard-of-ale have also been reproduced. Czechoslovakia seems to be the chief source, with the USA, Holland and Italy as runners-up. But a piece has to be valuable, much in demand or easy to make to be worth reproducing.

In general, modern glass is made of such highly refined materials as to be literally crystal clear and almost too brilliant, whereas any glass made before 1800 will normally display small air-bubbles against the light, and probably dark specks of impurities. Modern colours, also, are too vivid, whereas old coloured glass, especially blue, mellows with time. Clear glass tends to acquire a slight iridescence in humid conditions, and coloured glass a silvery glint—qualities that can be faked, however.

Soda glass can easily be told from lead under the utlra-violet lamp (see SODA GLASS). See also DRINKING GLASSES and specific examples of fakes under the appropriate entries.

Finger-bowls These were made from early in the 18th century. Some early ones had covers. Coloured varieties (blue, green, amethyst) appeared from the 1780s, the best heavily cut (fig. 35); and there are opaque white versions, gilded and marked 'Jacobs' (see BRISTOL). Some Irish bowls were mould-blown,

35 FINGER-BOWLS. Green bowl with gilding, Bristol (*City Art Gallery, Bristol*)

and modern replicas from the same moulds and marked 'Cork Glass Company' are misleading.

Fire polishing (1830s) A method of giving a bright polish to a finished product by briefly reheating it at the furnace mouth, thus partially re-melting the surface. This also eliminated pitting (caused by contact with the mould in MOULD-BLOWN and PRESSED GLASS), the ribs extruded through the joints of a mould in both these processes, and tool marks etc.

Firing glass (1740s) A sturdy DRAM, found with various types of bowl, especially the drawn trumpet, on a thick short stem (or stemless) and a very heavy foot considerably wider than the bowl-rim (fig. 36). It was intended for registering approbation by thumping on the table at club or Masonic meetings etc., and often appropriately engraved; **bumping** or

36 FIRING GLASS Enamelled by Beil in colour (*Cinzano Collection*)

37 FLASK. Gimmel flask, white stripes with blue rim, *c.* 1835 (*City Art Gallery, Bristol*)

hammering glass are alternative names for it. Terraced and square feet proved more vulnerable than a plain solid foot. Firing glasses were made up to mid 19th century; the name may derive from the noise they made, resembling musketry fire. **Ship's glasses** are identical in form, the heavy foot giving stability at sea. See also TUMBLER.

Flask Essentially a small narrow-necked flattened bottle, sometimes made for holster or pocket use; it might contain oil, wine, spirits or toilet water, and there is a wide range of shapes and styles, many in NAILSEA GLASS. The **gimmel flask** from French *jumelle*, 'twin') consisted of two flasks independently blown and fused together with necks pointing in opposite directions (fig. 37); provided with a foot it was used, even in the 17th century, for oil and vinegar, or for toilet water (fig.6). Most Nailsea examples have no foot and no discernible use. Another Nailsea curiosity is a close imitation of the small dressing-table bellows once used to powder one's wig (fig. 38); toilet waters were sold in these **bellows flasks.** For **pitkins** and **historical flasks** see AMERICAN GLASS.

Flute glass (1680s) A glass with a deep narrow conical or drawn trumpet bowl varying in height up to 14 but usually under 8 in. (20-35 cm). Flutes were made by the Dutch (fig. 39) in the 16th century; see also COMMEMORATIVE GLASS for the Exeter Flute. The early tall flute had to be made in soda glass as lead glass was too thick for this shape. Dwarf flutes continued to be made till the early 19th century.

The principal uses were for CHAMPAGNE, strong ale and cider, all of which precipitated sediment which sank to the narrow bottom out of harm's way. The engraving (often hops and barley) may distinguish ale from the rarer cider flutes. Stems were usually plain but there were some knopped air twists, and from *c.* 1830 rudimentary stems. For the flute cordial see **ratafia** under CORDIAL; see also TOASTING GLASS; YARD-OF-ALE.

Foot The foot of an 18th-century English drinking glass is almost always wider than the bowl rim and has the pontil mark of hand-blown wares (see MANU-FACTURING TECHNIQUES), which was left rough until *c.* 1780 (and sometimes on cheap glass until the 19th century) but thereafter usually ground and polished

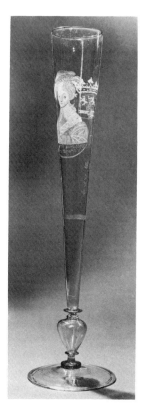

38 (*left*) FLASK. Bellows flask, pink and white; first half of 19th century (*City Art Gallery, Bristol*)

39 (*right*) FLUTE GLASS. Dutch diamond-point engraved, 'Wilhelmus Prince d'Orange' (i.e. William III of England as a boy), *c.* 1650 (*British Museum*)

into a smooth shallow depression on good quality glass—though even this feature disappeared *c.* 1850.

To keep the rough pontil mark from scratching the table, a domed or conical foot (figs 5 and 22) was necessary; and to protect the imperfectly annealed foot from chipping it was usual until the introduction of the 1745 tax, especially on balusters, to fold it back underneath forming a raised band (the **folded foot**; figs 21 and 26). The domed round foot was sometimes terraced in concentric tiers (fig. 28) and the solid square foot, which came into fashion in the 1770s, might be terraced and domed, domed or stepped. See also DRAMS; FIRING GLASS; RUMMERS; and fig. 50 ('lemon-squeezer').

French glass Apart from window and mirror glass there was little that was distinctively French before the 19th century, when France began to excel in OPALINE GLASS (1820s) and coloured glass. Prominent in later years were GALLÉ, LALIQUE and other artists of the ART NOUVEAU and ART DECO periods.

The chief glassworks were at Baccarat (1765) south-east of Nancy, St-Louis (1767) in the same region, and Clichy (1837) in a Paris suburb. The first two produced excellent cut lead glass. Baccarat also made SULPHIDES (1790s), moulded glass (with the name impressed inside the vessel), and blue, LITHYALIN and other coloured glass (1820s–50s). Clichy made yellow OVERLAYS, opaline glass and domestic wares. All made PAPERWEIGHTS.

Friggers The solemn official definition is 'fanciful articles made by glassblowers'. Americans call them 'whimseys' but the Scots win with 'whigmeleeries'. The term 'friggers', roughly, 'things made while mucking about', perpetuates the myth that they were made by glassmen in their spare time; but a 72-hour week in hothouse conditions would kill any urge to 'frig about' once the whistle went.

Friggers are traditionally attributed to NAILSEA, but most were made elsewhere. They are however in the typical Nailsea style, often with white or coloured loops etc; from *c.* 1845 some are in coloured lead glass. They were also made at fairs, in the market place or at the cottage door by freelance glassblowers armed with coloured glass rods and a little portable furnace or just an oil lamp. They thus make such things as small figures that can neither be blown nor moulded, simply by manipulating glass softened 'at the lamp' (fig. 40).

The typical frigger is gaudy, cheap, ingenious and, in most cases, quite useless and delightful. The chief categories included WALKING STICKS, BELLS, HATS, BOOTS, SHIPS, FLASKS and animals. Some testify to rustic superstitions (WITCH BALLS), some to the sweet

40 FRIGGERS. Group of small animals, *c.* 1835 (*City Art Gallery, Bristol*)

41 FRIGGERS. Bristol blown-glass dog-jug (*City Art Gallery, Bristol*)

sentimentalities which, in those days, seem to have been a sailors' monopoly only because most glasshouses were at seaports. ROLLING-PINS, scent bottles etc. inscribed with initials, dates (as early as 1809) and messages were exchanged between the sailor and his lass. Other toys were fair prizes, perhaps filled with hundreds-and-thousands or other goodies.

Friggers range from MINIATURE GLASS to monsters, e.g. 2 ft (0·6 m) TOBACCO PIPES, 3 ft (0·9 m) amber coaching horns (to represent brass), the YARD-OF-ALE and 4 ft (1·2 m) swords. Other oddities are dogs with curly glass hair, moving windmills, and elaborate set-pieces such as a fox-hunt with hounds in full cry—made this century (fig. 41).

Gadrooning A silversmith's term (from the French for 'puckered'), applied to moulded bands of heavy fluting, often wrythen, enclosing the base of a drinking-glass bowl (fig. 61) or other bowl as if in a cup.

Gallé, Émile (1846–1904)   The leading figure of the French ART NOUVEAU movement and of the Nancy school of design (in glass, furniture and pottery).   He was famous for CAMEO GLASS, first exhibited in 1889 in Paris.   This was made with two or more layers of coloured glass, the cameo work being entirely wheel-engraved on unique specimens, or with added acid-etching for 'limited editions', or entirely by acid for the commercial output.   Flower designs in non-naturalistic colours predominated (Plate 5) and to a lesser extent insects; Japanese inspiration is often evident.

The output of his factory was large and varied, including an opalescent pale blue *clair-de-lune* glass and cameo *vases parlants*, i.e. inscribed with lines from contemporary poets.   His pieces are signed but after his death his name continued to be used, with the addition of a star, on commercial lines of mainly uninspired vases with blue or mauve flowers on grey backgrounds.

German glass   The history of German glass inter-twines with that of BOHEMIAN GLASS.   Although the earliest North European glass was made in the Rhine-land, later improvements and innovations seem mostly to have spread from Nuremberg, which became to some extent a centre for the interchange of ideas and craftsmen between Hapsburg Bohemia-Silesia and the German states (of which there were some 350 in 1648).   Venetian craftsmanship was largely submerged by native traditions which suited less sophisticated local needs and tastes, especially for robustness, ostentation, a profusion of wheel-engraving and enamelling, and an idiosyncratic liking for fat stems bristling with PRUNTS; but above all for size—in Central Europe men drank beer rather than wine, and they drank deep.

From the early 15th century, and throughout the region, the well-named *Krautstrunk* was made—a straight-sided usually tall glass studded with prunts, giving the appearance of a stripped cabbage-stalk (hence the name). Also popular was the large *Humpen* (fig. 42), a covered beaker, normally very tall, made from *c.* 1550 both in Bavaria and its northern neighbour, Franconia. A Rhineland form, the *Passglas* (fig. 43), has three trailed horizontal bands, and was used either like the Bohemian *Vilkum* to welcome important visitors or perhaps to measure off quantities for a series of toasts. The *Waldglas* ROEMER was used everywhere.

The characteristic German surface wheel-ENGRAVING began with Caspar Lehmann (*c.* 1600) and their best ENAMEL PAINTING in the 1660s with Johann Schaper, both working in Nuremberg, where landscapes may perhaps be selected as most typical, whether enamelled or engraved. Another Nuremberg speciality was the very tall covered goblet (fig. 44) in *cristallo*, with stems lavishly knopped and collared, and the whole piece profusely engraved. The *Humpen* were favourites for enamel work, e.g. portraits of the Emperor and his Electors, or the imperial two-headed eagle, intended as presentation pieces for trade associations etc; usually they were dated. The *Passglas* was also enamelled, often with a playing-card. In the late 18th century Nuremberg, like Bohemia, turned to Neo-Classical wine and goblet shapes of greater simplicity. The enamelled *Humpen*, in particular, were reproduced late in the 19th century; they have covers (almost

42 (*above*)
GERMAN GLASS.
Humpen enamelled
with hunting scene,
late 16th century
(*British Museum*)

43 (*above*)
GERMAN GLASS.
Passglas enamelled
with triumphal
procession of an
Elector of Bavaria,
1662 (*British
Museum*)

44 (*left*) GERMAN
GLASS. Covered
goblet, engraved and
gilded; initials of
Peter the Great's
daughter, Empress
Elizabeth (1741–62)
(*British Museum*)

invariably lost in genuine ones) and no signs of wear.

In Potsdam, Kunckel made the first ruby glass (1679; see COLOURED GLASS) and about the same time Martin Winter introduced deep cutting (see ENGRAVING). After the 18th century supremacy in glassware finally passed to Bohemia.

Gilding Traces of gilding are found on early Roman glass; in Venice and Germany the gilding was sometimes 'gemmed' with dots of coloured enamel. This gilding was fired on after application; a later method, **oil gilding**, employing an adhesive, was more brilliant but less durable. In English **honey gilding** (from *c*. 1755) gold leaf was ground up with honey and, after light firing, burnished, but it still had rather a dull finish. A brassy finish resulted from **mercury gilding** ('best' gold), introduced *c*. 1790; in this the mercury of a gold amalgam was vaporized and the gilding burnished, proving relatively durable. From the 1850s **'bright'** or **liquid gold** was used, i.e. a very thin film of colloidal gold, so brilliant that it needed no burnishing. It did not wear well, but all gilding on glass is vulnerable.

Some English wines, ales and goblets, especially in the opaque-twist and facet-cut periods, were gilded with vines, hops or floral sprays, but in general gilding was rare except on colour, e.g. Bristol blue (Plate 2; fig. 93). A small fly in gilded designs is thought to be the 'trademark' of James Giles (see BRISTOL; Plate 2; fig. 79).

Glass, Ingredients of The essential ingredients of a **batch** (the mixture of raw materials ready to be fused into glass) are silicate (from sand) and a flux (usually soda or potash). The distinctive feature of

PLATE I

(below) AMBERINA. Pattern-moulded decanter, *c.* 1883–8, New England Glass Co. *(Corning Glass Museum)*

(above) Egyptian amphoriskos formed by the core method, 18th Dynasty, *c.* 1450–1350 *(Corning Glass Museum)*

(below) ART DECO. Sabino bowl, *c.* 1930 *(Sotheby's Belgravia)*

(*above left*) BRISTOL
Wine glass gilded
by Giles (*Harvey's
Museum*)

(*above right*) BRISTOL
BLUE. Vase with
Giles-decorated
bird (*City Art
Gallery, Bristol*)

PLATE 2

(*left*) BRISTOL BLUE.
Set of decanters in
silver stand (*City
Art Gallery, Bristol*)

(*above*) CAMEO GLASS. Two vases, *c.* 1888 (*Sotheby's Belgravia*)

PLATE 3

(*below*) BURMESE GLASS. Group of vases, *c.* 1890 (*Sotheby's Belgravia*)

PLATE 4

(*left*) DESSERT GLASSWARE
Épergne or centre-piece
in vaseline glass, *c.* 1850
(*Sotheby's Belgravia*)

(*right*) COLOUR TWISTS.
English 18th-century
wine; red, white and
green twist (*City Art
Gallery, Bristol*)

(above) FAÇON-DE-
VENISE. Salviati-
type ornaments,
c. 1900 (Sotheby's
Belgravia)

PLATE 5

(right) GALLÉ.
Vase, 1895
(Sotheby's Belgravia)

PLATE 6   LALIQUE.   Lamp, 1930 (*Sotheby's Belgravia*)

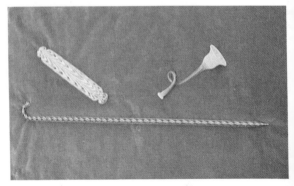

NAILSEA.   Nailsea-type walking stick, bugle and rolling-pin (*Mary Payton Antiques*)

PLATE 8

(*below*) TIFFANY GLASS. Poppy lamp
c. 1900 (*Sotheby's Belgravia*)

(*above*) PAPERWEIGHTS.
Isle of Wight sand-jar
(*Mary Payton Antiques*)

(*below*) SATIN GLASS.
Group of vases, *c.* 1880
(*Sotheby's Belgravia*)

'flint' glass is the addition of lead.

Sand for colourless glass must be as free as possible of impurities; the commonest of these is iron oxide which, present even in minute proportions, stains glass green. Sand therefore was taken only from selected regions, e.g. (in England) King's Lynn.

Soda, see SODA GLASS.

Potash, see POTASH GLASS.

Lime was present in the *barilla* used in the SODA GLASS made by the Venetians, who also added extra lime from other sources. Around 1700 the Bohemians added it to potash to produce a clear 'Bohemian crystal'.

Saltpetre (potassium nitrate) is a flux used e.g. in English lead glass, counteracting the yellow tint in it.

Lead added to a potash glass produces LEAD GLASS of great brilliance.

Arsenic is added to fine tableware to enhance brilliance and clarity.

Borax is now primarily used in ovenware, but also in some lead glass.

Decolorizers are added to offset unwanted tints caused by the impurities which cannot be wholly eliminated from the batch ingredients. In particular, manganese dioxide has been used since Roman times to offset contamination by iron, but it still left a faint tinge.

Cullet is broken glass-waste re-melted and re-used as part of a new batch; in shaping and trimming glass much of this fairly expensive material would otherwise have been wasted. It assisted the fusing process; as much as half of a lead-glass batch might be cullet, less in the finer wares as it affected clarity.

Glass, Repair of   Minor surface scratches e.g. on a paperweight can be removed with jeweller's rouge and a chamois leather; a more seriously damaged paperweight can be successfully repolished professionally but this alters the shape and lowers the value.   Any method of cleaning clouded or stained interiors of decanters and vases is liable to damage the glass by wearing away its surface—whether acid or lead-shot etc. is used.

Small chips in the rim or foot of a drinking glass can be ground out, but this may affect the balance and proportion of the glass and will always be detectable.

Glass pictures   These date from 1700 and continued into the 19th century.   After prolonged soaking, a mezzotint was laid face-down on a piece of glass coated with adhesive.   The paper was carefully sponged away, leaving only the black outline of the print on the glass; this was varnished over and painted in colour from the back.   The final product, resembling a delicately tinted engraving, was given a black-painted frame.

The earliest (all made in London) were portraits, but these were soon followed by sets of Seasons, Elements, or Continents (fig. 45).   By mid century transfers were being produced specifically for this purpose and there was mass production of pictures of outdoor sports, country scenes, allegorical themes etc., and commemorative pictures such as the death of Nelson or portraits of Queen Caroline and her daughter Charlotte; also religious pictures inspired by Wesleyan revivalism.   The genuine older examples (there have been forgeries) can be told by the slight irregularities

45 GLASS PICTURES. 'The Continents' (*J. & J. May*)

of the brittle early crown glass.

Some pictures were painted directly on to glass, e.g. 19th-century English marine subjects, well executed, as well as late Victorian landscapes and sentimental themes painted in crude colours. See VERRE ÉGLOMISÉ.

Goblet   A drinking glass with a bowl, usually round-funnel, large in proportion to stem-length, holding up to ¼ pt. (0·14 l) or more.   The earlier elaborate and covered types, Venetian in origin, have been dealt with under BOHEMIAN and GERMAN GLASS etc. English 18th-century goblets are found in combination with a wide range of stems and feet (figs 31 and 46).

99

46 (*left*) GOBLET. English baluster goblet, 1710; flared drawn trumpet bowl, solid at base; two angular knops; folded conical foot (*Alan Tillman Ltd*)

47 (*below*) HATS. Green splashed with white, *c.* 1835 (*City Art Gallery, Bristol*)

Hats A type of FRIGGER found in considerable variety, e.g. the beaver, 'stove-pipe', topper, bowler, jockey-cap, helmet, in clear or coloured glass (fig. 47), sometimes with Nailsea-type latticinio decoration. They must have been made primarily just for fun, but some were put to use for ink, mustard, toothpicks or even to snuff candles.

Hen-on-nest A late 19th-century version, nearly always in opaline glass, of the vividly coloured Staffordshire pottery nonsenses of the 1820s, probably used as fair prizes filled with sweets, as valentines or to hold Easter eggs. They range in size from about 10 in (25·4 cm) long to tiny miniatures.

Hollow stem (1745) A rare group of drinking glass, not very popular with collectors, many having large ungainly bowls and the fragile plain feet often being damaged. Knopped varieties on high domed feet may be Continental. There are some green and blue unknopped examples.

Sometimes called **excise glasses**, they may have been designed to lessen liability to the 1745 excise based on weight, or perhaps were simply a development from the elongated TEARS found in some PLAIN STRAIGHT STEM glasses.

Hour-glass A loose term for what is usually a sand (but may be a mercury) glass, measuring the elapse of various periods of time; the double bulb may be housed in silver, iron, wood, ivory etc. Three-minute egg-timers are still in use; others used to measure longer (much longer!) periods for sermons. Sets of four 'hour'-glasses in one frame measure quarters of an hour, cumulatively.

Hyalith A jet-black glass introduced in Bohemia (1822) in imitation of Wedgwood's black basalt stoneware (1767). It was developed mainly by Friedrich Egermann, who decorated it with gilt *chinoiserie* (fig. 48). Tableware, bowls, vases and scent bottles were made but the vogue was short-lived.

Incised twist (1750–65) A group of drinking glasses with stems incised on the surface with fine close spiral grooves; though rare they are not collectors' favourites. Knops are extremely rare; the unknopped ones often have large ungainly bowls.

Ink containers Handsome pairs of cut-glass inkwells were made as part of the furnishings of the elaborate 18th-century inkstandish; simpler versions may be found by themselves on a wooden stand. In the 19th century Stourbridge made elaborate inkpots in which the base both of the bottle and its large stopper is decorated in millefiori paperweight style (fig. 49). Some are made in the same type of bubbled pale green glass as is used in DUMPS, others in glass flecked with colours; and there are whimsical containers in the shape of a boot, boat, umbrella etc.

Irish glass The central dilemma in identifying Irish glass made during its heyday (c. 1780–1850) is that much of it came from glasshouses founded by English émigrés (Waterford, Belfast) or staffed by English craftsmen (Cork Glass Co.) or their Irish trainees; most of it was made to suit the tastes of the English market; and, except for marked pieces and those which resemble them closely enough, it is anybody's guess whether a given piece is Irish or English (or, for that matter, Scottish). (Fig. 50.)

48 (*left*) HYALITH.
Beaker gilded with
chinoiserie
(*Sotheby's*)

49 (*right*) INK
CONTAINERS. Ink-
bottle with millefiori
base and stopper in
red, pink, blue,
turquoise and white
(*City Art Gallery,
Bristol*)

A series of myths about Irish glass have been
demolished one after the other by later research,
until about all that remains is the view that the heavy,
thick-walled, deep-cut glass made up to 1825 is more
likely to be Irish than English because the untaxed
Irish could make it more cheaply. The hardiest
myth is that Waterford glass has a greyish-blue tint.
The truth is that most marked Waterford is remarkably clear, though some has the blue tint; but so has
much glass certainly attributable to other Irish and
English firms. It is thought to be due to the use of

50 IRISH GLASS. Fruit bowl, canoe-shaped with serrated rim; shallow diamonds, round lemon-squeezer base (*Sotheby's*)

lead from a particular Derbyshire mine, which imparted the colour until a means of eliminating it was discovered (by a Tipton firm) in 1810. Another theory is that it was simply due to excess of manganese decolorizer. Two other myths are in the Irish romantic tradition—that Irish glass has a more musical ring and a softer warmer feel. Decanters with three neck-rings and a mushroom or bull's-eye stopper are still obstinately called Irish (or even Waterford), but are not necessarily so—it was just a favourite pattern of the time. No particular cutting pattern can be safely attributed to Ireland, unless perhaps a greater use of curved motifs (difficult to execute) at Waterford.

Taxation and free trade shaped the career of Irish glass. The Excise Act of 1745 that taxed English glass also prohibited the export of glass from Ireland to England. This was a great blow to Ireland since the home market was small. The English tax was increased four times and this caused several English glassmakers to transfer their factories and workmen to Ireland, where there was no tax and where free trade was restored in 1780. Unfortunately, Irish glass was itself taxed in 1825, and one after another the firms failed, the last to survive being Waterford (1851).

Little is known of early Irish glass. Elizabeth granted a patent to an Englishman to set up a glasshouse in Co. Cork c. 1588; another was founded in Dublin c. 1690. Of the free-trade era firms the following are best known:

Waterford (1783–1851), founded by the Penrose brothers from Stourbridge, made all kinds of table (figs 20, 84–86) and ornamental ware and particularly fine chandeliers. Pieces marked 'Penrose Waterford' or with an engraved pen and rose include jugs, finger-bowls and decanters (fig. 25). The last were tapered or mallet-shaped with mushroom or bull's-eye stopper, short vertical flutes rising from the base, and shallow faceting on the shoulders. This firm was resuscitated in 1951 by the promoter of the Irish Sweepstake and is now a very large concern making exclusively hand-made wares according to old patterns.

Cork. The Cork Glass Co. (1783–1818) marked some of its products during its last seven years. The Waterloo Co. (1813–35) marked some of its decanters.

Dublin. Charles Mulvany (1785–1825) occasionally used the mark 'C.M.Co.'. The name 'Ayck-bowm' on some wares is thought to be of a Dublin retailer of the 1780s who sold the products of various glasshouses.

Belfast. A firm (1771–1829) founded by Benjamin Edwards of Bristol, who used the mark 'B. Edwards Belfast', made a wide range of glassware, including Bristol-type decanters.

The great fame of Irish glass has inspired considerable modern reproduction, usually with marks too legible to be genuine and the glass too heavy.

Jacobite glass (1746) The Jacobites were the Tories who after the Protestant William of Orange had come to the throne (1688) still wanted a restoration of the Catholic descendants of James II. Their activities came to a head in the Fifteen and the Forty-Five—the rebellions which failed to place on the throne either the Old Pretender, James's son (1715),

51 (*below left*) JACOBITE GLASS. Amen glass, diamond-engraved, *c.* 1750 (*Royal Scottish Museum*)
52 (*below right*) JACOBITE GLASS. Multiple-spiral air twist, bell bowl, conical foot (*Sotheby's*)

or the Young Pretender, his grandson (Bonnie Prince Charlie; died 1788) in 1745. It was a forlorn hope, fostered by the Pope and Louis XIV, but it led to the formation of numerous clandestine clubs whose members got a thrill from treasonably toasting the King Across the Water (not far across; both Pretenders took refuge in France and Rome).

It is surprising that so many Jacobite glasses are still auctioned; the answer is that many of them may be contemporary glass but their inscriptions are late and faked. Perfect fakes are being made to this day; others are betrayed by engraving too deep and white. Half the genuine survivors are air twists.

Jacobite (Latin *Jacobus*, 'James') symbolism ran riot. First came the very rare **Amen glasses** engraved in diamond-point with the earliest version of the National Anthem, ending 'Amen', 'IR' (James Rex'), a crown and the figure '8' (James VIII of Scotland); only 20 are known, engraved probably after Culloden (1746) on 1725 glasses (fig. 51). All the others are wheel-engraved (not very skilfully), usually with a rose (symbolizing the Crown) and one or two buds (for the Pretenders (figs 4 and 52)); or there may be portraits of the Pretenders (fig. 89). The commonest mottoes are *Fiat* ('May it come to pass'), *Redeat* ('May he return') and *Audentior Ibo* ('I go forward more boldly'). Other symbols are the star (of hope), butterfly, carnation, thistle and many others. These appear also on decanters, tumblers and finger-bowls.

Jugs **Cream and milk jugs** appear in great variety, sometimes matched with a sugar-bowl; the creamer has a wider lip than the milk jug. Some 1750 versions stood on three small feet; in Regency days there were deep-cut jugs, Neo-Classical silver shapes raised over a round foot, and miscellaneous coloured and clear jugs chiefly differentiated by handle shapes, though some had all-over latticinio designs in white with touches of blue and others were made in opaque white with coloured floral designs. 'Nailsea' jugs are found both in bottle-glass and coloured lead glass. There are plenty of cranberry jugs about and an occasional millefiori jug (fig. 62).

The typical glass **ewer** is a tall graceful jug, the slender body narrowing down to a circular foot, the long neck flaring out to a lipped mouth, and a decorative handle rising above rim-height. Venetian examples may be seen in museums. Some attractive ewers, made in opaline or frosted glass, decorated with enamelled floral or classical designs, gilding or black transfer-prints, came from Richardson of Stourbridge and Bacchus of Birmingham in the 1840s.

Flagon is not a very useful term in glass as it has been applied to such different shapes; it is properly a handled vessel with spout and lid (as in pewter). In glass the name was given to CLARET JUGS with round bellies, stoppered but lipless, but by mid-Victorian times it had acquired the wine-trade connotation of a flattened globular body, in which shape some claret jugs (with lips and stoppers) were made.

Water jugs during the Anglo-Irish period afforded an admirable opportunity for the glass-cutter to display his art at its best, later at its most elaborate, with every combination of different patterns on a single jug. Variations from the standard type include the ewer-shaped jug with a huge lip (1800); jugs with a ring foot (rather later); and coloured jugs (1845).

Kewblas (1890s) American three-layered glassware made to the formula clear over coloured over opaque white.

Knops Decorative swellings on the stems of drinking glasses and other stemmed vessels. It is impossible to put a date to the period during which any particular knop was in vogue. Pre-1700 English knops included the drop, angular (flattened cushion), annulated (flattened, usually with three sometimes even nine rings), bladed (flattened, with sharp edges), as well as the commonest forms on baluster stems, i.e. the ball, shoulder and flattened. A baluster glass dated *c.* 1700 has a cone knop between a (rare) cylinder and a drop knop.

Then came the cusp (wide angular), mushroom, dumb-bell, acorn and egg knops. There are often several knops on one stem and sometimes the whole stem is composed of knops only. Some knops contained tears or coins. The *merese* is a sharp-edged button connecting the stem with the bowl or foot.

Lalique glass Fancy moulded or pressed glass, usually opalescent or frosted, rarely coloured except for vaseline effects; made by Réné Lalique of Paris (1860–1945) and then by his son Marc. Réné was a designer of Art Nouveau jewellery but in 1908 turned to glassware and obtained a contract to make Coty's scent bottles. His best work belongs to the ART DECO 1920s and was mainly in the form of lamps (Plate 6), his glass usually showing its qualities only when illuminated. Isadora Duncan-type dancing figures were another popular line. In the 1930s the firm switched to commercial production of glass ashtrays, cigarette-boxes etc. Up to 1930 pieces were numbered and marked 'R. Lalique' sometimes plus 'France'; thereafter the 'R' was dropped.

Lamps In Ravenscroft's day lamps might consist of a hemp wick floating in whale oil in a lead-glass bowl mounted on a stem and circular foot; or a fixed wick protruding from a tube placed vertically in the centre of a covered bowl.

Lace-makers' lamps were used for close work (including engraving). They had bowls shaped like a bulbous lamp-chimney on footed stems, often with handles; the bowl was filled with water so that a candlestick placed behind it threw a diffused light on the workpiece. Some had a hollow stem and closed sphere instead of a bowl; this was filled with water through a hole in the base, which was corked; another type had two or four curved spouts (fig. 53).

53 LAMPS. Lace-maker's lamp with drip-pan under the bowl and a hollow inverted-baluster stem (*City Art Gallery, Bristol*)

54 LAMPS. Clarke's Novelty Fairy Lights (*Godden of Worthing Ltd*)

A great advance came in the 1780s with the **argand lamp**; this had the cylindrical wick and chimney with which we are familiar, and gave a much better light even using the rape-seed oil of the day; paraffin was not available until the 1860s—by which time domestic gas was widely used.

The font (reservoir) might be in cut glass, opaque white or coloured (including e.g. Burmese) glass; many are enamelled. The globes and shades, easily broken, are often replacements. Elaborate overlay table lamps with metal fittings and base were made in the 1860s. See also LALIQUE; TIFFANY.

Fairy lamps of decorative glass had a great but brief vogue from 1885, introduced to burn Samuel Clarke's long-lasting paraffin wax nightlights (fig. 54), and used not only in the nursery but at table and even as decorations for an outdoor evening function. The nightlight was put in a bowl (which bore the trademark of a fairy and such names as 'Wee Fairy'); the thimble-shaped glass shade was moulded in a great variety of designs and gave great scope for the use of Burmese and other coloured glass. More useful as illuminants were the clear-glass Cricklite shades

(1889), some on cut-glass or porcelain bases. There were many rival makes, with names such as Glowworm, one called hopefully The Burglar's Horror. Candelabrum and chandelier versions were also made.

Latticinio Decoration with opaque (originally milky white) threads embedded in clear glass; the threads were usually elaborated into gauze-like mesh, twisted cables etc. The term was soon extended to cover coloured threads. Latticinio was made by blowing clear glass into a mould lined with rods of opaque glass—a technique of Roman origin but perfected in 16th century Venice. Early specimens had single spaced threads (often 'pulled' into loops) but soon the walls of vessels (e.g. goblets) might be composed entirely of close-packed threads running continuously from bowl rim to edge of foot-rim (fig. 55).

One variant was to blow glass, with threads

55 LATTICINIO. Venetian bowl, mid 16th century; shallow fluted body, opaque white tapes and threads (*Alan Tillman Ltd*)

running diagonally, into another bulb of glass with threads running the other way, fusing to form a fine close network, called variously *vitro di trina* ('lace glass'), *reticello* ('network') or *Netzglas*. Another variant was the use of interwoven spirals of coloured and gold threads (**filigree**).

From these were developed (in England and Holland) the OPAQUE TWIST and COLOUR TWIST stems of drinking glasses, and the grounds of many paper-weights. Nailsea made much use of latticinio techniques. There have been many 19th and 20th-century reproductions of early designs. (Italian, from *latte*, 'milk'.)

Lattimo Opaque or semi-opaque milk-white glass, some of it opalescent, made in Venice from at least the 16th century, probably earlier, and gilded and painted. See MILK GLASS. (From Italian *latte*, 'milk'.)

Lead glass A term today (also 'lead crystal') applied to glass containing a substantial proportion of lead oxide. Historically, the addition of lead to a lime-free POTASH GLASS was George Ravenscroft's great contribution to glass-making (1675). It pro-duced a heavier, stronger, softer (and more easily scratched) and more readily fusible glass of much greater light-refractive brilliance than any of its predecessors, imparting a 'latent fire' effect. It could not be blown as thinly as Venetian soda glass but it was greatly valued both for its beauty unadorned and for its particular suitability for engraving and cutting; it gave, in open vessels, a sonorous ring, unlike most soda glass. There was no flint in it (see *Introduction*, pp. 18–19).

There were teething troubles; it was too brittle and the surface developed **crizzling**, i.e. a network of fine interior cracks which destroyed its transparency. A too-dusky tint was reduced when red lead was replaced by lead monoxide in the best quality wares. Other defects were specks and bubbles, variations in thickness, and if excess lead were present the surface turned dull grey with time. As the years passed these defects (virtues to the collector) were dealt with by improving the refining of materials, control of heating and methods of annealing, and by adding arsenic and decolorizers (see GLASS, INGREDIENTS OF). But entirely flawless, crystal-clear glass was not made until high-temperature gas-fired furnaces came into use in the 1850s.

In any pot of 'metal', the best came from the bottom, the poorest (*tale*) from the top; until *c.* 1800 the metal in the pots, though covered, was liable to be affected by furnace fumes. Quality today is indicated by such terms as 'full lead crystal' (35% lead) or 'half crystal'; 'flint glass' merely means colourless glass used in tablewares.

Lead glass was made in the late 18th century in Bohemia and at Lauenstein (Hanover), St Louis and Baccarat (France); the first American lead glass was made in Boston, 1813.

Lithyalin Opaque 'stone' glass imitating semi-precious and other stones, e.g. agate, jasper, usually marbled in red, blue-red, blue-green, green-yellow. It was patented *c.* 1828 in Bohemia by Friedrich Egermann, but soon imitated elsewhere (fig. 56). He made vases, scent and cologne bottles etc. in it.

Lustre vases A mid 19th-century development from the pendant-hung candlestick, which became a widely popular mantelpiece ornament in late Victorian and

56 (*above*)
LITHYALIN. *Left to
right:* pale amethyst
marbled goblet;
seven-sided beaker
simulating agate;
opalescent Persian-
blue marbled goblet
(*Christie's*)

57 (*left*) LUSTRE
VASES. Mid-
Victorian vase
(*Godden of Worthing
Ltd*)

58 LYNN GLASS.
Opaque twist stem
(*Christie's*)

Edwardian times. Completely non-functional, they held neither candle nor flowers, the candle-socket having become a bowl, usually with serrated edge, often (like the stem and foot) in cased glass, from the rim or base of which hung a circle of long pendant lustres which tinkled in a draught (fig. 57).

The word 'lustre' has to be treated with care, as it can mean 'chandelier', 'pendant' or 'lustre vase', or refer to the lustre in ceramic lustrewares.

Lynn glass   A high-quality drinking glass (including ales and tumblers) or decanter, decorated with several rows of horizontal ribbing. Most of the surviving wine glasses have opaque-twist stems (fig. 58) and some have folded feet.   They are thought to have been made in Norfolk, either in King's Lynn (hence the name) or Norwich, perhaps 1720–80.

Manufacturing techniques   There are two basic methods of making glass hollow-ware—by blowing (in use since the beginning of the Christian era; see *Introduction*, pp. 10–11) or by pressing (invented *c.* 1825; see PRESSED GLASS).   Blown glass was, from the earliest days, either **free-blown** (i.e. shaped without the use of a mould) or blown into a mould to give it shape and/or decoration (see MOULD-BLOWN GLASS). The processes used in blowing glass are, in essentials, much the same now as 2000 years ago.

A hollow iron tube, the **blowing iron**, is dipped into the furnace hole to collect a blob (**gather**) of molten glass (**metal**) on its belled-out end.   Being of a treacly consistency, the 'metal' sticks to the iron when withdrawn from the furnace, but cools quickly enough for it to be rolled almost immediately to and fro on a polished steel table (**marver**) to smooth its surface.   It is then ready to be inflated, as a soap bubble is blown—the glassworker controlling size and shape by the duration and intensity of his blowing, and by rotating the iron as he blows.   The resultant bubble may be further rolled, further inflated, swung to and fro to elongate it, or held vertically while the still plastic glass gradually changes shape under the force of gravity.

The blowing iron is then detached by touching the glass with water or a moistened tool and giving it a sharp tap, causing a clean break.   For handling during the finishing processes, a solid iron rod, the **pontil rod** (or punty rod), is attached to the glass.   The **pontil mark** is the scar left on earlier glass when the pontil rod is similarly broken off.   Until *c.* 1780 vessels intended for table use had a domed foot or a **kick** (indentation) in the base to keep the rough scar from scratching it; thereafter it was polished smooth.

External features (e.g. handles) and final shape are added by the **gaffer**, sitting in a **gaffer's chair** with wide flat arms on which the blowing iron or pontil rod is rotated as he works; he has a battery of tools to hand, e.g. shears and scissors for trimming the rim of bowl or foot of a drinking glass. At various stages the rapidly cooling glass is reheated at the **glory-hole**, a mouth of the furnace, to keep it plastic and workable. See also PINCHED WORK.

The finished article is then put in the **annealing tunnel** (*lehr*, also spelt *leer*, from the German for 'empty oven'), where it is gradually cooled and toughened. Unless annealed, glass is easily shattered and there was much wastage in manufacture (and breakage in use) until this process was mastered; the cause—uneven cooling—is the same that produces firecracks in porcelain. An annealing kiln was used in England until *c.* 1750, when the much more effective German tunnel was adopted, through which the glass was very slowly drawn for at least 24 hours. An improved lehr was introduced *c.* 1780.

These operations, in various combinations, are carried out by a team (**chair**) of men, each with specialized functions, under the gaffer; they pass the glass on its tube or rod from one to another or place it on a bed of mechanically operated rollers—constant rotation being essential to ensure that the plastic shape is not distorted. Stripped to the waist, the men weave rhythmically to and fro, from furnace to marver, from gaffer's chair to lehr, with the disciplined precision of an intricate, endlessly repeated ballet. The unconscious choreography of the scene cannot fail to impress the lay observer.

Great skill is required at all stages to achieve and retain symmetry. Features of early 18th-century glass are the minor differences between the items of a matching set and variations in the thickness of a bowl.

Glass components in the plastic state can readily be fused to each other, the join being almost imperceptible. Thus, for example, in making a three-piece (**stuck-shank**) wine glass the bowl is shaped first, the independently formed stem is then stuck on to it and finally the foot is added. Unfortunately, this means that today a rare old bowl or stem can be given a foot from another glass as a replacement.

A typical furnace may contain many separate pots, some containing the best metal for the highest quality glass, others a coloured metal. The greater the heat the better the metal in freedom from bubbles, striations and specks; a great improvement in this respect came with the Perrott furnace (1738). (See also GLASS, INGREDIENTS OF.)

Marbles Even Venetian children played with hand-blown glass marbles, probably not dissimilar to those in use in this century, with their gaudy enamel spirals. The most decorative are the 18th-century varieties made for the solitaire board. Most 19th-century marbles came from Nuremberg. There is a wide range of colouration and some are made of opaque or crackle glass.

Mary Gregory glass Originally made by a Bohemian export firm (1850–80), in clear or coloured glass enamelled in white with pictures of children at play, dressed in the mode of the day and country of origin (fig. 59). It had a vogue in America where it was much copied, and attributed to a decorator named Mary Gregory for whose existence there is no evidence.

Later even cruder imitations were made (and are still made), decorated in coloured enamels, with flesh tints. Jugs, vases, decanters etc. were so decorated, some inscribed 'A present from . . .'; probably none of it is English.

Masonic glass The establishment of the Grand Lodge of England (1717) marked the beginnings of modern Freemasonry there. Early symbols engraved on 18th-century glass (especially on FIRING GLASSES) included the beehive (industriousness) and ladder. In addition to the square, trowel and compass (with the motto 'Keep within Compass'), there was the all-seeing eye of God, 'G' in overlapping triangles, and Classical columns (for stability of character), among others. (Fig. 61.)

Mead A glass with an incurved globular GADROONED bowl on a tall or medium stem is thought by some to have been intended for mead, the fermented honey and water (or ale) drink (fig. 60). The strongest form, metheglin, with added spices and herbs, was the favoured tipple in Tara's halls.

Milk glass A name for glass rendered opaque white by the addition of tin oxide. Owing to natural confusion with *Milchglas* and LATTIMO, some kinds of both of which are better described as early forms of OPALINE GLASS, the more precise alternative, OPAQUE WHITE GLASS, is preferable.

The name is also sometimes given to Victorian translucent white glass ornaments made mostly in England, USA and Germany throughout the 19th century, often hand-painted or in pressed glass.

Millefiori A type of MOSAIC GLASS decoration used

59 (*above*) MARY GREGORY GLASS. (*Mary Payton Antiques*)

60 (*below*) MEAD. Early English gadrooned specimen (*Christie's*)

61 (*left*) MASONIC GLASS. Cup with stem containing a coin dated 1813. On the opposite side is engraved a hop-and-barley design and the monogram 'HET' (*By permission of the Board of General Purposes, United Grand Lodge of England*)

in Venice and revived in the mid 19th-century French and English paperweights. Quarter-inch sections are cut from $\frac{1}{4}$ in (6·3 mm) diameter rods made from layers of different coloured glass, patterned to resemble stylized flower-heads, stars etc., the same pattern running right through the rod as in Brighton Rock. The sections are arranged in patterns on the bed of the paperweight.

Embedded in clear glass, closely packed or spaced out, such patterns may also form the base or sides of tumblers, finger-bowls, jugs (fig. 62) and vases, or be used in inkpots (Stourbridge; fig. 49), door-knobs, scent bottles, buttons etc. (Italian, 'thousand flowers'.)

Miniature glass Glass toys were made in England from the late 17th century, and particularly in Birmingham from *c.* 1750, some for doll's houses, some for adults. Enormous trouble was obviously taken with some pieces, e.g. goldfish swimming in spun glass, a tiny opaque-twist wine glass, a blue liqueur glass engraved with a hunting scene, tiny scent bottles in animal form, 'Venetian' glass, complete tea-sets etc. Quantities were imported from Germany and Bohemia, and Art Nouveau glassmen also made miniature toys.

Mirrors Silvered glass was made in Venice from the 13th, in Nuremberg from the 14th century. In Tudor England mirrors of polished metal were used unless glass ones could be imported (at high cost) from France or Italy; but in 1618 Mansell started making small mirrors of **broad sheet** glass (see WINDOW GLASS). They gave a rather hazy, dark but deep reflection. The glass was thin, the bevelling wide and very shallow. The thickness of the glass can be

62 MILLEFIORI.
(*Mary Payton Antiques*)

gauged from the apparent distance between the edge of a coin, placed on its surface, and its reflection. Larger **plate glass** mirrors could be made from the 1770s.

Until 1848 mirrors were 'silvered' with mercury backed by tinfoil; then a (much cheaper) thin coating of silver was substituted. The presence of the familiar reddish-brown substance on the back indicates a post-1850 mirror or an older one re-silvered. The silvering, spotting or other imperfections of a genuine old mirror can be faked, but the white-coloured glass may give things away.

The French **chimney-glass** or **overmantel** was introduced to England in the 18th century and was at first long and in three separate pieces, later square, then tall; many were decorated by Dutch artists with floral, landscape, *chinoiserie* or even sporting themes. The **pier glass** was another early 18th-century introduction, placed against the 'pier' walls between windows. The **cheval glass,** a full-length mirror swivelling on a 'horse', came to England *c.* 1800. It developed from the dressing-table or **toilet mirror**, which also swivelled, and might stand on a base fitted with drawers. Small circular **convex mirrors** were made in Germany from the 15th and introduced to England in the 18th century, usually surmounted by a gesso eagle. Sometimes called **butler's mirrors**, they were said to enable the servants in a large room to keep an unobtrusive eye on the need to replenish glasses, say, and presumably the mistress to keep a more obtrusive eye on servants or children; in any case, they cheered the room up. See also SILVERED GLASS.

Mixed twist (1750–65) A stem with a combination of air and opaque twists. This type is rather rarer than the colour twist. The commonest form is a wine glass with opaque-white gauze surrounded by a pair of air spirals (fig. 87); knops are very rare.

Mosaic glass Small sections of coloured glass rods fused together, usually on to a flat backing surface, to form a design. The best examples were made in Alexandria at the beginning of the Christian era, and the Romans decorated their bathroom walls with them; the technique was revived in Venice. Mosaic glass was also re-heated and moulded into simple shapes. The coloured rods could be sliced up to use in inlays or as beads. MILLEFIORI is a specific form of mosaic glass.

Mould-blown glass Syrians blew glass into a mould, and the technique has been used ever since. The mould, at first of clay and from the 1750s of gunmetal, may be used simply to shape the glass or to impress on it patterns cut into the mould's inner surface or for both purposes. It may be the shape and size of the finished article; or part-size, the glass being blown into it to give it decoration (and initial shape) and then withdrawn to be further blown to full size. The latter method does not distort the pattern, but the edges (e.g. of an imitation cut-glass pattern) are softened; the American term for this is **pattern-moulded** (Plate 1).

The earliest moulds were one-piece, which imposed limitations on the shape of the finished product and on the kind of decoration. For example, the lower part of many 18th-century decanters was blown into a **dip mould** cut with vertical flutes or ribs. These had to be vertical, not horizontal, and the decanter had to taper, if only slightly, towards the base—otherwise it could not be withdrawn from the mould. One trick was to twist the piece as it was withdrawn from a ribbed mould, giving a **wrythen** pattern (swirled moulding, often seen on ale glasses). One-piece moulds were much used in the 18th century to make wine bottles (after they became cylindrical) and some decanters.

To overcome these limitations a hinged **two-piece mould** was used by the Venetians and Dutch in the 16th century; a greatly improved form was invented at Stourbridge in 1802, by which any kind of pattern could be impressed and many shapes accommodated. For more complicated shapes **three-piece** (c. 1820) and **four-piece** moulds were used.

Glass blown into these moulds extruded through the slight gaps between the hinged sections, forming (unwanted) ribs on the surface. From the 1830s these were partly or wholly removed by FIRE POLISHING.

The glass remained of uniform width in section, which meant that each convex rib on the surface was matched by a corresponding concavity inside, and vice versa (creating, incidentally, cleansing problems in decanters). This is the great difference between mould-blown and PRESSED GLASS; the latter is smooth inside. These interior mouldings were less marked, of course, when the vessel was blown into a part-size mould and then further inflated—they may be mere ripples. Mould-blown glass is thinner and clearer than pressed glass, but the patterns are less sharp, though they may be finished by wheel-cutting.

Blown-three-mould is an American term for a range of cheap wares (1815–35), classified according to pattern-motifs.

Blown moulding was mechanized in the 1840s and also to a large extent outmoded by pressed glass.

Nailsea (1788–1873) A glass-making centre 8 miles (13 km) west of Bristol which in its heyday was chiefly known for its excellent crown window-glass. Later, the same cheap window-glass was used for everyday domestic wares (jugs, mugs, flasks), and from 1815 for what are better classified as FRIGGERS. The early Nailsea wares (e.g. ROLLING PINS) were decorated with flecks or mottling in white or in bright colours (yellow and red being the rarest). The mottling was done by rolling the glass over chips of coloured enamel. The most typical product, however, was clear glass with loops of colour or white made by the LATTICINIO technique, i.e. glass was blown into moulds in which canes of coloured glass (pink, yellow, blue, ruby, green) had been arranged, the stripes being manipulated ('pulled') into curved patterns during further blowing. (Plate 6).

The majority of so-called Nailsea friggers, however, were not made at Nailsea but at numerous other centres, e.g. as far away as Newcastle and Alloa.

Newcastle drinking glasses (1735–65) The collector's joy, a group of beautifully proportioned three-piece glasses made at Newcastle upon Tyne in a particularly brilliant metal; known also as **light balusters.** Very light, with waisted round-funnel bowls, tall slender stems and complex combinations of knops, which usually contained collections of tiny TEARS, they are almost all wheel or stipple engraved, often by Dutch engravers (fig. 63), sometimes by Norwegians; others have enamelling attributed to BEILBY. Too fragile to survive in quantity, they are rare and expensive today; the inevitable fakes should not deceive.

63 NEWCASTLE DRINKING GLASSES. Round-funnel bowl diamond-point engraved with the arms of the wife of William V of Orange (reigned 1766–95) (*Sotheby's*)

Opaline glass Generic term for several kinds of semi-opaque white or coloured glass which usually shows a fiery opalescence when held to the light, due to admixture with bone-ash, arsenic, fluorspar, or zirconium etc; also called **opal glass**. Colours ranged from greyish cream ('alabaster') to apple green and later to yellow, ruby, blue etc. Some kinds were painted and gilded and many were given a matt surface with acid.

The fashion was set by French vases and urns of Classical shape (1827), usually mounted in ormolu. Other types came from Spain, Bohemia (in overlay) and elsewhere.

The Richardsons of Stourbridge made 'vitrified enamel' vases (fig. 64), some Athenian in shape and decoration (Plate 7), and Sowerby (Newcastle) produced elaborate art glass in this medium, as did Lalique. American **onyx glass**, in pink and amber, is opalescent.

Opaque twist (1755) A group of glasses, often called **cotton twists**, with stems in which spiralling threads are formed by canes of opaque white enamel glass instead of the air of AIR TWISTS. The forms and combinations are the same as for air twists with the addition of spiral tapes (very wide flattened threads) and laces (spiral lace-like single bands, often heavily outlined at the edges); there are over 140 varieties of design. Nearly all opaque twists are three-piece glasses with plain feet; folded feet are rare.

About three-quarters are unknopped double-series (figs 5, 10, 21), with a very wide variety of twists. Many are engraved (fig. 65) or enamelled. English examples are much whiter than the Dutch; genuine

64 (*left*) OPALINE
GLASS. Richardson
vitrified enamel vase,
c. 1850 (*Godden of
Worthing Ltd*)

65 (*right*) OPAQUE
TWIST. English wheel-
engraved wine, 1760
(*Royal Scottish
Museum*)

glasses have the twist extending the whole length of the stem. The 1777 tax on opaque 'enamel' glass may have put paid to their production; there was a revived vogue for them in the 19th century. See also LYNN GLASS.

Opaque white glass Glass rendered opaque by the addition of tin oxide. For its antecedents and alternative names see ENAMEL GLASS; LATTIMO; MILK GLASS.

In the 1720s the potentialities of white glass as a cheaper substitute for porcelain began to be recognized. Painted in enamel colours or transfer-printed, it could be made to resemble porcelain very closely; by 1722 the German chemist Johann Kunckel was already calling it 'porcelain glass' and German and Bohemian glasshouses were exporting it in quantity to England.

Unfortunately, the tin oxide caused extreme fragility. In the 1750s, using improved annealing methods to toughen it, English firms began to make it, probably first at Bristol and soon afterwards at Warrington, King's Lynn, Sunderland and elsewhere. To give it greater density, a higher than normal lead content was used; this made it soft and easily defaced by black scratches, and heat resistance was also too low for some domestic uses. The final blow came in 1777, when excise duty added to its already high cost, ending its ability to compete with porcelain.

Bristol 18th-century opaque white is now extremely rare; decorated pieces are usually attributed to Michael Edkins (see BRISTOL) on slender grounds. The Warrington-made products are thought to have been transfer-printed in black by Sadler & Green, a Liverpool firm better known for work on pottery and porcelain. Some of the enamel painting was done by

experienced ceramic artists. A wide range of porcelain
shapes and patterns were made, as candlesticks, scent
bottles (figs 78 and 79), vases, tea-caddies (fig. 66) etc.
Some genuine pieces have been redecorated in modern
times; there are also reproductions.

Overlay Strictly speaking, overlay and **flashed glass**
are different forms of **cased glass**, but they are
frequently confused and involve much the same
techniques, and so are conveniently dealt with together.

There are two or more layers of glass, the inner one
usually clear and the others in contrasting colours or
opaque white. These are blown successively inside
one another and fused together. Slanting cuts are
made through the outer layers to make 'windows' or
other patterns edged with the various colours thereby
revealed. This technique, Roman in origin, was

revived on a commercial scale in Bohemia *c.* 1815; it became widely known and popular abroad partly through being sold at spas such as Carlsbad, where in fact some of it was made. The process cannot be applied to mould-blown or pressed glass.

Decanters, drinking glasses (with cased bowls, and stems in yet another colour for good measure) and cologne bottles were among the commonest forms. The 19th-century glassmakers, rarely given to leaving well alone, would add engravings and paintings of castles, hunting and rural scenes etc., and even the clear-glass 'windows' might be embellished. The technique was also much used in paperweights.

The most popular Bohemian colour combinations were ruby on clear, and opaque white on ruby or rosaline (rose-pink), the white being enamel-painted in floral and other designs. English glassworkers, notably the Richardsons of Stourbridge (*c.* 1845), used up to five layers of the heavier lead glass, cut deep; colours include reds, greens, blues, and yellow (gold). Vases, rare in Bohemia, were an English speciality (Plate 7 and fig. 67); the drinking glasses had thicker feet than the Bohemian.

Flashed glass was of two kinds—with the coloured layer simply surface-stained (usually ruby; see STAINED GLASS) or with a clear glass dipped in molten coloured glass before blowing. The cutting needed to be only very shallow; sometimes the outer layer was merely etched away.

Much reproduction cased (especially flashed) glass was made in Czechoslovakia between the wars and is still made (fig. 68). Generally speaking it looks as new as it is, and the patterns have a mechanical regularity. See also CAMEO GLASS.

67 (*above*) OVERLAY.
Group of 'Bohemian'
vases. 1850
(*Sotheby's Belgravia*)

68 (*right*) OVERLAY.
Decanter flashed ruby
(*Mary Payton
Antiques*)

Paperweights These are so various they need a book to themselves. The earliest progenitor seems to have been the 15th-century Venetian millefiori doorstop, and MILLEFIORI remains the commonest design. To make this (taking one of numerous variations in the process), the thin slices of multi-coloured rods are arranged in the required pattern face-down on a concave metal plate; this constitutes the **set-up**, over which a mould is placed and filled with molten glass to form the base of the weight. The other side is then repeatedly dipped in clear glass until a high solid dome is built up over the set-up. The dome greatly magnifies the design and enhances its colouring, so it is important that it should be of flawless glass. The canes, which may be **florets** (many-coloured stylized flowers) or enclose tiny **silhouettes** of animals etc., may be arranged against a coloured or opaque white ground, in close, concentric or scattered patterns, in mushroom tufts (a sheaf of canes 'tied' with coloured glass or ensconced in a 'basket'), or scrambled (*macédoine*, **pell-mell**—bits of broken cane).

There are many varieties of ground; LATTICINIO grounds are usually white but may be coloured, arranged as lace, muslin, gauze or 'upset latticinio' (scattered fragments). Other grounds are the **carpet** of tightly packed miniature canes; **stardust**, of star-shaped canes; **honeycomb** etc. The other main categories of design include single flowers, bouquets, fruit, vegetables, insects, reptiles and SULPHIDES. Some of these may be cased in OVERLAYS cut with one central window and usually five more round the side. The average width of a weight is about 3 in (7·2cm); **magnums** and **miniatures** are about 1 in (2·5 cm) wider or narrower.

By far the best weights came from three French factories in the 1840s and 1850s: Baccarat, using superb lead glass; St-Louis, also in lead glass; and Clichy, which by some miracle achieved equal brilliance with a boracic/soda formula. All three made optical glass—hence the high standards. (For these factories, see FRENCH GLASS.)

Baccarat weights are mainly millefiori (about two-thirds of the output), at which they excelled. Some of these are close millefiori (fig. 69a) and are dated (on canes); many are also signed 'B' or have various silhouettes as trademark. The commonest date is 1848, the rarest 1849; a few are dated 1846 or 1847; no other dates occur. The dates on old French paper-

69 PAPERWEIGHTS. a. Baccarat millefiori marked 'B 1848'; b. St-Louis, faceted, with floral spray; c. Clichy swirl in blue and white (*City Art Gallery, Bristol*)

weights should be at the side, never central, and are sometimes difficult to spot. Baccarat dates usually have the outside digits in red, the inside blue and the 'B' green. The commonest silhouettes are the broad arrow and 'Swiss roll'; others are animal, bird, fish, insect, flower or, very rarely, a devil. The other weights are mainly flower designs, especially primrose, pansy, clematis. There are few, but excellent, overlays, usually blue over white, with millefiori set-ups. The rarest feature reptiles on a rock ground, or butterflies.

Half the **St-Louis** weights are millefiori (including mushroom, concentric and scrambled) or flowers (fig. 69b), in about equal quantity. Silhouettes include the camel, dog, birds and dancing figures. Some are signed 'SL' with or without dates (the same dates as Baccarat); usually the first three digits are black, the last red, and 1848 is again the commonest. In the flower and fruit section, dahlias and fuchsias are most prized, also bouquets, and there are many pears, cherries and even the turnip (so French!). There is a higher proportion of snakes and lizards (on white latticinio), and an extremely rare salamander. The overlays are usually in blue, green or pink. In general, colours are less vivid than those of rival firms. St-Louis also made the only hollow-blown weights ('**crown weights**').

Clichy made some of the best weights, and in later years some of the worst; they also had the brightest colours, and preferred millefiori (about 80%) to more exotic designs, the best being scattered, mushroom or garlands, the least attractive and commonest being scrambled on a background unenthusiastically dubbed 'sodden snow'. Some have a signature 'C' in black, red or green; a very few are marked 'Clichy'; none are dated. The Clichy rose is a frequent 'signature', usually pink with an outer ring of green petals. Flower subjects, very rare, include single roses and pansies. The few snakes are on lace grounds. An attractive speciality is the **swirl** (about 10%; fig. 69c), with spirals of alternate white and one colour (turquoise, purple, green). There are a few excellent double overlays (turquoise, rose or green over white) and some sulphides of very varied quality. A unique Clichy feature is the slightly concave base with a broad flat frosted border.

Under the ultra-violet lamp Baccarat shows blue, St-Louis pink, Clichy green.

English weights of the same period are mostly millefiori or floral and for the most part inferior to French; the metal is rather cloudy. The best come from George Bacchus of Birmingham. These were wider and had larger canes than the French, and the design tended to fill the weight; pastel colours predominate. Bacchus made the first English overlay weights (1851).

Stourbridge weights, made by three firms, had a minute, sometimes beaded, foot, and the concentric millefiori designs, viewed sideways, are flat; colours tended to be crude—red, blue and white. Stourbridge is however more famous for its fine millefiori inkwells (see INK CONTAINERS), vases, egg-shaped hand-coolers, TUMBLERS, scent bottles, DUMPS, rulers etc.

Other English weights of the period came from Apsley PELLATT and the Islington Glass Works. In the 1860s came a vogue for small **pictorial weights**, simply a coloured print or engraving of a seaside or

70 PAPERWEIGHTS. Pictorial weights (*Godden of Worthing Ltd*)

other resort stuck on to the base of a dome of glass (fig. 70).

Another curiosity is a **sand-filled weight** in the form of a lighthouse (Plate 8), bell or swan, made from the 1840s. The fine-grained many-coloured sands of Alum Bay (Isle of Wight) were ingeniously used to depict delicately coloured and detailed local scenes (e.g. the Needles). These were sold as 'trifles' to holiday visitors and, filled to the brim and stoppered up, miraculously retain their designs to this day.

There is an enormous variety of **modern paperweights**, the best by Paul Ysart, working in Scotland, some signed 'P.Y.' on canes. Whitefriars until recently made concentric millefiori overlays, good copies of early Stourbridge, and contemporary commemorative weights (e.g. the Queen's coronation).

In the USA original designs and copies of the French were made and there are several moderns, the best perhaps being Whittemore, Gentile and Kazium.

Since 1920 indifferent reproductions have come from Czechoslovakia, Japan, China and Venice. Baccarat from 1953 made excellent sulphides (Churchill, Roosevelt, Lincoln) and poor millefiori, signed on the base. Earlier a man named Dupont working at Baccarat in the 1930s made some remarkably good reproductions (especially pansies) and is probably responsible for those bearing such unlikely dates as 1815. Baccarat's St-Louis factory are still making excellent sulphides, fruit, flower and commemorative weights, some marked 'SL 1952' etc.

In general, fakes can be told by their lack of weight and patina and their uneven set-ups (especially when viewed sideways). Artificial signs of wear and 'ageing' with acid do not disguise the modernity of the glass used.

Pâte-de-verre Powdered clear or coloured glass mixed to a paste with water and gum, used by the Egyptians. It could be heated and fused to form a rough-surfaced dense body, moulded like potter's clay or carved like stoneware. Its use was revived during the Art Nouveau and Art Deco periods to make masks, panels etc.

Peachblow (1880s) American glass with shaded colours like BURMESE GLASS, made by many firms and imitated in England by Thomas Webb and Stevens & Williams. The colours may be red shading to yellow, blue or cream etc. and the surface may be given a satin (matt) finish. Peachblow was first made to imitate the glaze on a famous piece of Chinese porcelain.

Pellatt, Apsley (1791–1863) A glassmaker who, at his father's glassworks in Southwark, perfected the SULPHIDE (1819), and in 1848 was the first in England to make Baccarat-style millefiori paperweights. In 1849 he published *Curiosities of Glassmaking*; by then he had also become a voluble Liberal MP.

Pinched work Applied ornament or components of a glass object which can more conveniently be made separately, often by specialists—e.g. stoppers, finials, lustre drops, PRUNTS, pinched trailing (i.e. a notched ribbon of glass). Various hand-tools were used, e.g. pincers fitted with metal discs incised with the design required. The square **lemon-squeezer foot** of a rummer might be hand-pressed into a one-piece mould.

A design of the Ravenscroft period, called **nipt-diamond-waies** and probably borrowed from the Low Countries, consists of horizontal or vertical applied ribbing pincered together to form a wide-mesh diamond network, partly or wholly covering drinking-glass bowls, punch bowls etc.

Plain Straight Stems (1710–60) Nearly a quarter of English 18th-century drinking glasses fall into this category; they are mostly two-piece glasses, varying greatly in quality and in shape of bowl. Although intended for the cheaper market, many of the earlier examples, especially goblets, have pleasing proportions. Nearly half of them have trumpet bowls; the next commonest are waisted and ogee. Stems vary from very slender TOASTING GLASS type to very thick (thought to be Irish), and TEARS are common; as the name implies, there are no knops.

Collectors tend to neglect all except early drawn

71 POMONA. Vase, *c.* 1885–88. New England Glass Co. (*Corning Glass Museum*)

trumpets on folded feet, glasses with well-formed tears, and engraved **electioneering goblets** (given away by candidates).

Pomona (1886) American STAINED GLASS, typically amber (sometimes blue), part of which is decorated with a network of finely etched lines, usually with added floral (especially cornflower) decoration (fig. 71). A cheaper variety was made by rolling the glass in acid-resistant material and etching the unprotected areas.

Portland Vase (AD 100) The most famous example of CAMEO GLASS, a two-handled urn with a thick layer of opaque white glass cut away to reveal a dark-blue ground, against which stand in bold relief figures depicting the story of the sea-goddess Thetis and her

human husband, father of Achilles. It was found in a sarcophagus near Rome in the 17th century, later brought to England, sold to the Duchess of Portland, lent to the British Museum where an Irish madman smashed it (1845), reassembled, auctioned in 1929 (withdrawn at 29,000 gns) and finally bought for the British Museum in 1946.

Wedgwood copied it in jasperware (1790) and first revealed that it was made of glass not stone. Northwood made a replica of it in glass (1876).

Posset and caudle glassware Posset pots were spouted pots with two handles and a cover, made in pottery and in glass from *c.* 1680 possibly until 1800; three survivors have the Ravenscroft seal. A smaller posset glass was made from 1700, resembling a two-handed jelly glass but with a spout (fig. 72). Posset was hot spiced milk curdled with ale or wine, plus breadcrumbs—apparently a kill-or-cure for colds.

Pottery **caudle cups** (1750s) had no spout, but there seems to have been no similar development in glass; a vessel like a glass teapot with handle and spout at right-angles was probably used for caudle from c. 1800. Caudle (from the Latin for 'hot') was a hot thin gruel, sweetened, spiced and laced with wine or spirits as a pick-me-up for nursing mothers and invalids.

Potash glass Potash, the chief alternative to soda as an alkaline flux, was obtained from wood-ash in old German *Waldglas* and from bracken in the similar French *verre-de-fougère* (see *Introduction*, p. 12). Potash glass cools and hardens very quickly, unlike SODA GLASS, allowing very little time for manipulation. It is harder and more brilliant than soda glass (and also more expensive); necessarily thick in section, it was particularly suitable for the deep engraving found on BOHEMIAN GLASS, especially after lime was added to it to form 'Bohemian crystal'; it also takes a good polish. Potash (without lime) was also used in LEAD GLASS.

Potichomania Briefly, pasting coloured transfer-designs inside glass vessels to make them look like enamelled porcelain. Also called **decalcomania**, large names for a minor craze which originated in Paris; variously described as an aristocratic pastime of the 1800s, the poor man's do-it-yourself Meissen and (by Dickens) 'a pretty lady-like accomplishment of considerable variety and application'. Printed designs were bought for a few pence, but fixing them on the inside of a vase with a narrow neck must have been tiresome; so in the 1880s the 'maniacs' started pasting them outside pottery vases. The final stage was to decorate these with cigar-bands.

French *potiche* is a vase of classical Chinese shape. French *décalquer* is to transfer an impression on transfer-paper from a (calcareous) lithographic stone.

73 PRESSED GLASS. Modern American powder box made from old moulds; lid tinted yellow (*City Art Gallery, Bristol*)

Pressed glass (1825) An American invention for the mass production of a cheap substitute for mould-blown and cut-glass tableware. First exploited on a large scale by Deming Jarves at the Boston & Sandwich Glass Works, it was once called **Sandwich glass**.

As in MOULD-BLOWN GLASS, two, three or four-piece moulds were used; these were heated and molten glass poured into them in exactly calculated quantities. A vertical plunger rammed the glass against the patterned mould, leaving the interior of the vessel smooth (in contrast to mould-blown ware). This method was at once copied by other American factories, but as the glass had to be thick it was not much used in England until after excise was abolished (1845).

Most early American pressed glass (**lacy glass**) had intricate all-over patterns (daisy, heart, star, hobnail) in the style of embroidery, any gaps in the design being filled with **stippling**, i.e. tiny raised dots which gave a distinctive silvery sparkle to the general appearance and concealed defects. Bits of glass often stuck to the mould, causing surface pitting and variations in brilliance, a characteristic until the 1860s. Some blemishes could be removed by FIRE POLISHING, including the seams of glass extruded through the mould sections (thinner than those in mould-blown glass).

In America from the 1840s sets of tableware were made in matching patterns (marked with names such as 'Excelsior', 'Waffle'); those which had no stippling are sometimes called **pattern glass** (fig. 73). In England the two chief centres were Co. Durham and the Midlands; wares often bore a REGISTRATION MARK and a trademark, e.g. a peacock (Sowerby), lion rampant (Greener of Sunderland), lion with axe (Davidson of Gateshead). Sowerby's **vitro-porcelain**, meant to look like porcelain, was pressed into small ornaments, the most frequently seen being baskets in turquoise. American pressed glass and English cut-glass patterns were both copied; products included commemorative plates, jugs and candlesticks, together with vast quantities of custard and jelly glasses, sets of coloured dessert plates, cup-plates, cream jugs, butter dishes, wine glasses, hens-on-nest, swans, vases-in-hand and other vases, boots etc. These were made in lead, slag and potash-lime glass, in clear, coloured or opaque white glass. Such wares are still reproduced in Victorian styles today.

Compared with mould-blown glass, pressed glass was thick and dull (especially on the inner surface). The patterns were not ordinarily as sharply defined as hand-cut glass (though more mechanically regular), but some were touched up at the cutting wheel, giving the brilliance of cut glass—only to the parts so treated, however. In later years patterns became over-elaborate, in the late Victorian taste, and in such high relief that cleaning presented problems.

Prunts A German speciality from the earliest times to today, taking the form of applied prickly bosses of glass moulded or stamped into various forms (the commonest being the 'raspberry' prunt) or drawn out into curved spikes; the Germans aptly call them 'warts'. The vogue had spread all over Northern Europe by the 15th century. They were placed all round the *Krautstrunk* beakers and some other types of GERMAN GLASS (fig. 74); in the ubiquitous ROEMERS the very thick hollow stem is a mass of prunts, possibly to hide the dregs of Rhenish wine or to get a good grip on late in the evening. Some goblets have small prunts three-quarters and half way down the side of the bowl as marks down to which toasts were drunk. In England prunts (fig. 77) appear on Ravenscroft goblets and on some Nailsea glass.

Punch glasses (1690s) Punch was ladled out of

74 (*right*) PRUNTS.
Stangenglas (narrow
Humpen on pedestal
foot), with rows of
prunts inside and out;
probably Rhineland,
early 16th century
(*British Museum*)

75 (*left*) PUNCH
GLASSES. English
punch-bowl, *c.* 1800;
height 13 in
(33·5 cm) (*City Art
Gallery, Bristol*)

punch bowls into, probably, a variety of glasses, e.g. rummers, drawn trumpets, handled tumblers (**cans**) or the cup-bowled or double-ogee bowled stemless **bonnet-glasses** sometimes confusingly called **monteiths** (see WINE-GLASS COOLER); the last, some in blue glass, may in fact have been salts or sweetmeats.

The bowls were usually of silver or porcelain; glass bowls, often engraved, had a short, knopped stem on a domed and folded foot (fig. 75) or, from the 1750s, a rudimentary stem or shallow base.

In late 17th-century England punch was a spiced and sweetened mixture of brandy, rum or wine with fruit juices, usually served hot.

Registration marks Some pressed glass bears a registration mark, a diamond surmounted by III (for Class III, glass), with a year letter at the top corner (1842–67) or at the right-hand angle (1868–83); or a registration number only, starting at 1 in 1884, reaching 100,000 in 1889, 300,000 in 1898, 500,000 in 1908. The mark gives the date the pattern was registered, not the date of manufacture.

Roemer A stocky wine goblet, associated with Rhenish wines and still used for hock in Rhineland cafés, with a large bowl shaped like three-quarters of a sphere, and an enormously thick cylindrical stem, short, studded with PRUNTS all round, and hollow, originally so that the profuse sediment of Rhenish wine could sink into it (fig. 76). The foot was conical, later pedestal.

Presumably first made in the Rhineland, it became popular in the Low Countries in the 16th century (hence the Dutch spelling; German *Römer*, probably meaning 'Roman') before it was adopted elsewhere.

76 ROEMER.
Spherical bowl, wide
hollow stem with
raspberry prunts, and
coil-wound foot;
17th century
(*Sotheby's*)

In 17th-century England it was used also for sack, claret and beer; some were made by Ravenscroft. See RUMMER.

Rolling-pins (1790s) Nailsea-type FRIGGERS made in great quantity, especially at ports, and widely reproduced in this century. The earliest were solid, with knobs at each end; later ones were hollow, stoppered at one end. As every housewife knows, hot hands never made good pastry, and glass (solid or filled with cold water) would help; hollow Pyrex rolling-pins are sold today. They are said to have numerous other uses: to hold or smuggle salt, sugar, tea, rum; to hold the family will, or sweets (as fairings); as decorations, lucky charms, lovers' tokens.

The inscriptions range from 'I love a sailor' and biblical texts to a mariner's *cri-de-coeur*: 'And from great guns and women's tongues, Good Lord, deliver me!'; and the pictorial ones from hare-coursing to ships and Sunderland Bridge. The themes are predominantly nautical—some commemorate naval battles.

The rolling-pins came in all the Nailsea styles of decoration—flecked or mottled colours, latticinio loops—Bristol blue; gilded, enamelled, transfer-printed; in bottle or lead glass (Plate 6).

Rudimentary and short stems The largest and most miscellaneous class of drinking glass, featuring every kind of bowl and foot; rummers predominate. Jelly glasses (see DESSERT GLASSWARE) have knops instead of stems; rummers, dwarf ales and drams may have short stems, either knopped or plain.

Rummer (1770s) In general, a large-capacity goblet with ovoid bowl, short stem and sturdy foot, used for long drinks such as rum and water, toddy, punch and beer. The name has no connection with rum but is a 17th-century anglicization of ROEMER, a type of glass which was copied in England (fig. 77).

The rummer was still being made at the end of the 19th century, and in this long period took many shapes—the bowl might be bucket-shaped, the foot round or a heavy square 'lemon-squeezer' base; the metal and workmanship ranged from high quality to poor. Decoration might be hand-cut, mould-blown or engraved (especially as commemorative glass). See also TODDY-RUMMER.

Salts Silver salts were being copied in glass before

77 RUMMER. Early example with prunts, perhaps attributable to Hawley Bishopp; 1681–85 (*Royal Scottish Museum*)

1700 and thereafter appeared in widely differing shapes, e.g. circular dishes with three feet; canoe or boat shaped on an oval foot (1770s); double-ogee bowl, sometimes scalloped, on short, sometimes knopped stem and circular foot (1790s–1850s); canoe-shaped with notched rim on square foot; deeply cut; mould-blown in colour; sets of Irish salts which were minia-ture copies of their canoe dishes (see fig. 50).

In 1835 the very high salt tax was lifted and the use of pressed glass salt cellars became widespread, at first plain rectangular and from 1850 copying early shapes. In the 1880s slag-glass salts were typically in blue, with serrated rim and terraced square foot.

Satin glass (1880s) Glass with a remarkably silky feel to it, the surface made matt by steeping it in acid vapour; the name could be applied e.g. to PEACHBLOW but more specifically refers to glass with a mould-blown opaque white 'lining' dipped in coloured glass; this is also called **mother-of-pearl glass**. Cream jugs, vases (Plate 8), lampshades and rose-bowls are favourite pieces, sometimes in shaded tones of pink, yellow, blue etc. (e.g. BURMESE GLASS). There are also diamond-quilted and similar patterns (see CAMEO GLASS), an effect obtained by trapping air-pockets between the outer layer and the moulded concavities of the white core. Satin glass was made in America, Stourbridge and elsewhere.

Scent bottles A term here used to cover the vast range of containers for scents, toilet waters, smelling salts etc. One of the oldest forms of glassware, scent

78 SCENT BOTTLES.
Bristol opaque white,
London decorated,
gold screw cover
(*Christie's*)

79 SCENT BOTTLES. Two blue, two opaque white, all gilded in the manner of James Giles; later 18th century (*City Art Gallery, Bristol*)

bottles were made in Egypt, Venice and eventually almost everywhere. The best English examples date from the 18th century. The essential features are that they should be small, airtight and in coloured glass, for scent deteriorates not only in air but in light. Ground-in stoppers, further protected by hinged or screw tops of gold, silver, pewter etc., were desirable safeguards; the bottles were made in blue, green or opaque white, the last with enamel decoration (figs 78 and 79), and cut glass was much used from *c.* 1780. Other forms of 19th-century decorative treatment include overlay, sulphides, cameo glass, millefiori and lithyalin. Shapes are equally varied, e.g. acorn, shell, boot, negro's head. Larger bottles were made for cologne, lavender and other toilet waters for use at the dressing-table.

Vinaigrettes or **smelling bottles** had an ornamental grille holding in a sponge steeped in aromatic vinegar, or contained smelling salts (sal volatile); these were invaluable amid the prevailing stenches of 18th-century urban life, and also brought Victorian young ladies round from the 'vapours' to which they were so prone. Vinaigrettes were more often in metal or porcelain, but some were in deep-cut thick glass and intermediate in size between scent and toilet-water bottles; the glass is permanently corroded by its contents. **Double-ended scent bottles** were a mid-Victorian speciality, holding handkerchief scent at one end, smelling salts at the other.

'**Oxford lavenders**' are long thin containers of thick-walled square section with stoppers (now usually missing) and crudely made, mostly in the 19th century; their capacity is so minute that their purpose is a puzzle. They were made on the Continent, some think in Germany for the Bulgarian attar of roses trade.

Ships Sailing ships with coloured SPUN-GLASS rigging and other details, sometimes complete with crew and tossing on a sea of foaming glass, were made from the late 18th century. An old example in good condition is rarely found.

Ships-in-bottles were made throughout the 19th century. The sea, of painted cork etc., was pushed in first and glued down. The wooden ship, with masts flat on the deck, was then inserted; threads pulled the masts and top hamper vertical.

Silesian stem (1715–50) A shape of stem, also called **Moulded Pedestal** or **Shouldered**, found not only on drinking glasses (fig. 80) but on sweetmeats (figs 19 and 26) and candlesticks, either semi-hollow or with a long TEAR, and moulded with four, six or eight sides, the last being the latest and commonest of a rare group; some are in poor lead or soda metal. See

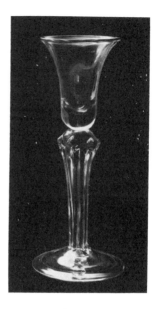

80 SILESIAN STEM. Bell bowl on tall star-studded hexagonal stem; folded conical foot (*Sotheby's*)

also CHAMPAGNE.

Some early examples had 'G.R.', a crown or 'God Save King George' moulded on the shoulders, and refer to the accession of George I of Hanover (1714).

Silvered glass   (1) In the 1850s, tableware etc. with double walls between which a silver nitrate solution was poured, giving the appearance of solid silver. There were attractive goblets and vases made in this way, including some additionally embellished with engraving, gilding or flashing over with colour which was cut away to reveal a pattern against the silver background.   Much silvered glass is, however, of poor quality. (2) In the 1870s, glass on which silver was deposited to give a filigree effect.

Slag glass (1840s) Opaque PRESSED GLASS with streaks of colour, especially purple and white (called **purple slag**), the colour being due to the addition of slag taken from the surface of molten steel. It was first developed by Sowerby of Gateshead and was also made in America. The slag was cheap and increased durability. Tableware and vases were the chief products (fig. 81).

Blue, green, brown and orange, all mottled with white, are also found. **End-of-day glass** is another nickname, attributed to the fact that slag was drawn off at the end of the steelworkers' shift.

Marble glass is similar, used in covered dishes, cakestands etc., e.g. in black, cream, mulberry, tortoiseshell (the last two rare). All these types are still being made in Victorian styles today.

Soda glass The earliest form of glass, and still made today, in which the flux is soda, not potash. The Ancient Egyptians obtained their soda in the form of natron from dried-up lakes. Spanish *barilla*, from burnt salt-marsh plants (e.g. glasswort), contained soda and lime, and this (or its near relatives) was used in Mediterranean countries, notably in VENETIAN GLASS, while potash glass was developed in Central Europe. From the 16th century Spain also exported *barilla* to Antwerp and England for use in Venetian-style glass (*façon-de-Venise*); it was used in England up to Ravenscroft's time. In more durable forms than the Venetian, soda glass continued to be made in England (as elsewhere) after lead glass came in. In general, 18th-century soda glass was lighter, less

81 SLAG GLASS. North Country slagware, 1876–82
(*Godden of Worthing Ltd*)

resonant, less lustrous, more likely to be flawed by bubbles, specks and colour tints. But some lead glass had all these deficiencies, while some soda glass had none of them, was very well made and might be almost indistinguishable from lead. The final arbiter is the ultra-violet lamp, under which soda glass shows yellow and lead blue. Fakers of lead glass may use soda glass but counteract the light weight by thickening the base of the bowl etc.

The important distinctive property of soda glass is that it has a lower melting point than potash glass and cools more slowly (remains plastic longer), thus giving more time for manipulation (as in the Venetian fantasies), and more easily blown, moulded or spun.

Spangle glass (1880s) American flecked glass made by rolling the molten metal over flaked or powdered silver, gold (rare), mica or AVENTURINE etc., and subsequently casing it in clear glass. Glittering silvery pink vessels with crystal handles were popular as fairings; blue flecked with silver was another combination. Spangle glass was also made in Bohemia and at Stourbridge.

Spatter glass (1880s) An American glass, also called **Splash glass**, streaked with variegated colours; molten glass (coloured or opaque white) was rolled over fragments of coloured glass instead of the metallic flakes used for SPANGLE GLASS. Vases and bowls were made with many combinations of mottled colours.

Spun glass Glass fibre was spun in Roman times but is now only of industrial importance. In the 19th century, however, it appeared in some Nailsea-type fantasies, e.g. glass ships floated on waves of it and glass goldfish swam in it.   Other curiosities were knottable neckties and whole gowns spun for e.g. an actress and a Spanish *infanta*—though whether they could sit down in them is not recorded.

Stained glass   The glass in medieval church windows was normally stained with metallic oxides in the usual way; but if this would produce too dark an effect, e.g. with ruby, the colour was flashed on to clear glass (see OVERLAY) and might be etched.   The figures or designs were outlined by the lead framework and details added in various ways.   After the 16th century 'the bastard art of painted glass' came in.   The new Coventry Cathedral reverted to medieval methods.

   Stained glass tableware was first made (1830s) in Bohemia, a thin film of metallic oxide being applied to a finished clear glass, inside or out, and then refired. Similar glass, usually in ruby or bright green, was made at Stourbridge in the 1840s.   It was a useful method for colouring cheap pressed or mould-blown glass, which could not be flashed in the normal way.

Stems   English 18th-century drinking glasses are classified by their stems.   In chronological order, these are: Baluster and Balustroid, Plain Straight, Silesian, Newcastle, Air Twist, Composite, Hollow, Incised Twist, Mixed Twist, Colour Twist, Opaque Twist, Faceted.   There are separate entries for all these.   See also RUDIMENTARY AND SHORT STEMS.

Stirrup-cup   Originally 'one for the road', a drink handed to a guest when mounted and ready to depart. With charming logicality, the stirrup-cup glass is left footless, there being nothing one could do with it except empty it and hand it back to the footman.

Stirrup-cups were also used at inns to hand to coach passengers during a brief halt (and hence called **coaching glasses**), and at meets.

The bowl and stem were sturdy, even clumsy, but otherwise followed contemporary fashions, and the thick stem was rounded off, perhaps with a ball knop; unfortunately an ordinary glass with a broken foot can easily be converted, though the lack of robustness should give it away. Most survivors are 19th-century.

Sulphide A ceramic low-relief cameo embedded in clear glass; also called *crystallo-ceramie*, glass-encrusted cameo, cameo incrustation. An 18th-century French invention, copied in Bohemia, it is chiefly associated with the name of Apsley PELLATT who perfected the

82 SULPHIDE. Baccarat tumbler, 1830–50 (*Cinzano Collection*)

process in 1819, overcoming the difficulties of ensuring that the glass did not distort the cameo and eliminating unequal expansion and contraction of the two components by using a specially prepared ceramic mixture based on china clay (which produced the characteristic silvery effect). Sulphides were expensive.

The cameos were at first mainly portraits of royalty and other celebrities (fig. 82), and coats-of-arms; later there were landscapes, cupids, mythological scenes etc. Sulphide decoration appeared in medallions, plaques, decanters, vases, candlesticks, drinking glasses, scent bottles and even in the stems of sweetmeats; but particularly in PAPERWEIGHTS. Baccarat paperweight cameos depicted Joan of Arc, royalty, myths, sporting scenes (and in modern times J. F. Kennedy and the Queen), and Clichy portrait busts only.

Most early cameos were beautifully made and the glass of the clearest. From mid century there was a decline in quality except for those made in Edinburgh by John Ford (1870s–80s). **Medallion inlays** were an imitation in which an intaglio impression in the base replaced the sulphide and the glass was polished on top but left cloudy inside, to get the silvery effect.

Syllabub glass (1725) A large glass with a double-ogee bowl, the rim very wide and the lower part sometimes exceptionally deep on a rudimentary stem; others with a normal bowl on a normal knopped stem. Sweetened spiced wine was poured into the bottom and covered over with a frothy concoction of cream, dry wine and lemon juice.

This was the form in which ladies of the early Hanoverian era took syllabub. There are numerous differing recipes from the 16th to 19th centuries,

83 TABLE GLASS. Anglo-Irish canoe-shaped salad bowl, cut glass, *c.* 1800 (*Royal Scottish Museum*)

mentioning every kind of alcohol from brandy to cider. The syllabub glass probably gave way in time to the much smaller jelly glass.

Table glass The very best Georgian glass was entirely hand-blown and hand-tooled, but most of the rest was at least partly mould-blown. In general, the earlier heavier shapes began to yield place to thinner-blown, shallow-cut wares in the 1740s and then to the deep-cut pieces of the Anglo-Irish period. Matching sets came into vogue in the 1840s in coloured glass, later in pressed glass.

In addition to DESSERT GLASS, JUGS, DRINKING GLASSES and DECANTERS, there is a wide range of

84 TABLE GLASS. Waterford 'kettle-drum' fruit bowl, c. 1785 (*National Museum of Ireland*)

collectable items of table glass, of which the following merit separate mention:

Glass **baskets** descended from their épergnes (see DESSERT GLASS) in the 1850s to be placed up and down the dining table filled with fruit or posies. They are found in various forms of pressed glass moulded with basket-weave patterns, and later in slag in shapes that effectively prevent their holding anything.

Bowls. (1) **Fruit and salad bowls** were a favourite medium for the Anglo-Irish cut-glass specialists; later examples might combine cut and moulded decoration or be (from 1820) wholly moulded. Three striking shapes predominate: the oval **canoe** (or boat; 1770–1820; fig. 83); the circular bowl with a massive

turned-over rim which was heavily cut; and the **kettle-drum** (1820–40), a deeper, more vertically sided bowl, also with heavy turnover (fig. 84). Rims that were not turned over were serrated or scalloped in various patterns (shell, fan, etc.). The bowls might stand on three quite large feet (1770s), or on a sturdy circular or square base; the substantial short stem might be knopped. See also FINGER-BOWL; PUNCH GLASSES.

(2) **Sugar bowls** belong mostly to the 19th century. Some, looking like oversize widened-out egg-cups, are in opaque white of the Bristol type, enamelled with a floral pattern or inscribed, in gilt, 'Be Canny with the Sugar'; they may have a matching cream jug. Others are in cut blue glass with or without a silver rim and handle; the distinctive Anglo-Irish turnover rim is also found, above a cut square base. Many bowls are boldly cut (fig. 85) or gadrooned.

Celery vases, large, tall, on short or rudimentary stems and spreading feet, are found from the late 18th century, in cut or mould-blown glass (fig. 86). The turnover rim again recurs.

Cruets and castors are confusing terms. Originally 'cruet' meant a stoppered bottle for oil, vinegar etc., and castors were bottles with perforated tops of silver or other metal, to sprinkle sugar or pepper. Both 'cruet' and 'the castors' have been used in the past for the stands which held them. Similarly, 'condiments' is used not only of seasoning and sauces (especially salt, pepper, mustard) but of their containers. The 18th-century bottles might be mallet, pear, cylinder or urn shaped, and most later versions were in cut glass. There was a wide range

85 (*above*) TABLE GLASS. Waterford sugar bowl, *c.* 1810 (*National Museum of Ireland*)

86 (*left*) TABLE GLASS. Waterford celery glass, *c.* 1820 (*National Museum of Ireland*)

of Victorian pressed-glass mustard pots; see also SALTS. Probably the most admired condiment bottles are sets of BRISTOL BLUE or opaque white labelled bottles.

Cups and saucers were made in Venice in the 18th century in opaque white glass with enamelled decoration. An attractive set (attributed to Bristol, 1790) has a white latticinio pattern and blue rim, and is matched with a sugar bowl.

A **cup plate** was used to put the cup on when tea was cooled in and drunk from the real saucer; the three pieces were sold as a trio. Slightly smaller than a tea-plate, the cup plate is found in lacy pressed glass and later in coloured glass. This way of drinking tea had become 'provincial' in the 1820s, and was also copied in America.

Knife-rests are commoner in metal and pottery, but dumb-bell shapes are found in cut lead glass, and Stourbridge in the 19th century produced some decorated with millefiori or colour twists. The original purpose was to keep the used knife and fork off the table while the courses were changed—one kept the same implements throughout the meal.

Lacy-patterned **plates** were among the earliest pressed glass wares, some with serrated edges to their rims. A coronation souvenir of 1838 has a portrait of the Queen with various inscriptions. **Ice plates** are deep dishes with a wide rim used in Regency times to serve water ices (sorbets); made in clear glass, often with a Greek key pattern, or in deep ruby with a star-cut or frosted base.

An occasional **tea caddy** is found, a glass version of a silver shape, e.g. in Bristol blue, octagonal (or, rather, rectangular with sliced-off corners), cut with flutes and mounted with Sheffield plate (c. 1790);

in Bristol opaque white in enamel colours, labelled for different kinds of tea (Green, Black, Bohea, Hyson); or in flattened whisky-flask shape.

The **teaspoon-holder** is a squat, stemmed goblet, in clear, coloured, often pressed, glass. In early Victorian days one took one's own spoon from it (as in canteens today). If the bowl is deep, it is probably a **spill-holder**.

Tankard A large, footed mug, in its silver or pewter form usually lidded. In glass, tankards range from early Dutch and Bohemian versions (a few fitted with metal lids) to those in Bristol blue or Nailsea-type speckled designs. The body is often waisted or bell-shaped, occasionally ovoid; sometimes there is gadrooning round the base, moulded floral decoration or engraving (e.g. with hops and barley on ale tankards). Some are COIN GLASSES.

Taxation In 1745 lead glass was taxed at a penny a pound weight; this excise duty was raised four times until it reached $10\frac{1}{2}d$ a pound in 1820, plus an annual fee of £20 per furnace. The excise was abolished in 1845.

There is still disagreement on the extent to which taxation affected the ingredients used (e.g. less lead, lighter weight), or the shapes (hollow stems, smaller size, disappearance of folded feet, shallow cutting) or led to compensatory embellishment (twist stems, engraving, enamelling, gilding) or impeded innovations (e.g. overlays, coloured glass). Some think that these changes (in so far as they are not imaginary) can be attributed to changing tastes, improved furnaces and annealing.

It was, however, not so much the weight of

taxation that hampered the industry as its administration; drunken, ignorant and corrupt excisemen held up production by checking and weighing the glass at each stage of its manufacture. In 1851 a newspaper reported; 'England is behind all Europe in glass manufacture owing to excise *supervision* and tax. Its abolition has had the most satisfactory results.' Ireland was exempt until 1825, with important consequences for the industry (see IRISH GLASS). Bottle-glass was taxed at much lower rates.

Tear bottles Bottles resembling 'Oxford lavenders' (with which they have been confused; see SCENT BOTTLES) but much shorter, found in graves and made by the Chinese and the Syrians. They probably held (niggardly) quantities of oil or scent, but a romantic tradition has it that one wept into them at the funeral—an excessively difficult exercise.

Tears Air-bubbles intentionally inserted in the stem of a glass or in the solid base of its bowl. The best are symmetrically pear-shaped tear-drops, others may be lopsided or quite shapeless cavities. Possibly the air twist developed from the elongated tear which sometimes extends all along the stem. Tears are commonest in the Plain Straight Stem; in Newcastle light balusters there are groups of tiny tears inside the knops ('**beaded knops**').

To make them, the surface of the glass, while still plastic, was dented with a metal instrument and the hole covered over with more glass, trapping air. The air-bubble expanded with heat and was drawn into shape.

Tiffany glass Fancy, coloured glass made in the

glasshouses of Louis Comfort Tiffany (1848–1933), artist son of New York's famous jeweller, and leader in the US of the Art Nouveau movement. Tiffany revived old techniques and devised new, but the most popular was his **favrile** glass (a coined word vaguely suggesting 'hand-made'), first exhibited in 1893. This had an iridescent satiny finish imparted by metallic salts atomized in the kiln, and is found in various shades of blue, ruby, green, mauve, bronze, mother-of-pearl etc.

This glass was blown into (mainly non-functional) vases suggesting elongated shapes of plant life—e.g. the tulip vase on a tall ultra-thin stem—or into more

87 TOASTING GLASS. Drawn trumpet, mixed twist, opaque gauze core and spiral air twist (*Christie's*)

conventional shapes embellished with e.g. peacock-feather stripes or inlaid decoration. Another popular category is formed by lamps with dragon-fly, water-lily etc. motifs (Plate 8); these, like other products of the period, were seen at their best only when lit. There were also figures with drapery and flesh tints indicated by coloured glass.

Many pieces are signed 'L.C.T.' or 'Tiffany-favrile', with a serial number. Imitation presented little difficulty and has been widely practised in USA, Bohemia, France and Austria.

Toasting glass (1690s) A drawn-trumpet glass with a tall and extremely slender stem, usually in soda glass as it was meant to be snapped in two after toasting the 'King across the Water' or other celebrity (fig. 87). Naturally, few survive.

Those with fatter stems are sometimes called **semi-toasting glasses**; they can hardly have been meant for snapping—some even having air-twist stems.

Toastmaster's glass (1740s) A CORDIAL or wine glass with a normal-sized bowl outwardly, but cunningly thick sides which reduced capacity to as little as a sixth of normal, thus guarding the toastmaster against hangovers; often engraved, and made in the best glass. For **sham drams** see DRAM.

Tobacco pipes Large glass pipes, some as much as a yard long, were first used as shop-signs outside tobacconists' and as tavern ornaments. In early Victorian times they became cottage ornaments too, in various shapes and usually with long solid stems furnished with knop-like swellings. Some were decorated with spirals of colour or opaque white,

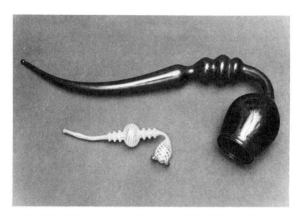

88 TOBACCO PIPES. Ruby glass pipe, 16½ in (41·8 cm);
small pipe, white stripes with blue rim; *c.* 1835 (*City Art
Gallery, Bristol*)

others were in plain coloured lead glass, the latter
sometimes having hollow stems (fig. 88).

Toddy-rummer (1780s)   A giant 1½ pt (0·85 l)
thick-walled RUMMER in which hot toddy was prepared. This might be transferred to individual
rummers (or tumblers) by **toddy-lifter**, a small
pipette-style vessel shaped like a miniature decanter
and filled through a hole in its base—the contents
being held there during transfer by placing a finger
over the mouth of the 'decanter'.

Sugar was put in each glass and stirred with a
toddy-stick (or **sugar-crusher**), a 5 in (12·7 cm)
glass pestle, which might be cut, incised or have an
ornamental finial.

Hot toddy was a 50:50 mixture of rum and hot

water sweetened and flavoured with lemon and nutmeg; from the very early 19th century other spirits might be substituted for rum, and toddy became a favourite Victorian drink.

Trick glasses Tavern humour was exercised through the YARD-OF-ALE and the BOOT GLASS; also to be found are wines and tumblers so decorated as to conceal holes near the rim likely to incommode the drinker—but there was nothing so elaborate as the Staffordshire pottery puzzle-jug.

Tumbler A development from the BEAKER that owes its odd name to a silver predecessor with a rounded base (which therefore 'tumbled'). Usually it has straight sides sloping slightly inwards to the base (fig. 89) but some, e.g. from Yarmouth, are barrel-shaped. Squat tumblers were used in the 17th century for strong beer or brandy; those of normal size date from the 1750s and were often engraved, e.g. with regimental badges, Masonic symbols, hops, ships, famous steeplechases, named horses; or inscribed for a wedding or christening, or to a hunt etc. Some were enamelled (fig. 30) or gilded. (See also fig. 82.)

There were also 19th-century **thumping glasses** or **bumpers** with thick solid bases, successors to the FIRING GLASS; some had three dice loose in the base, to determine the perennial problem of who is to stand the next round. Stourbridge (1850s) added millefiori bases, and there were short cut-glass Regency tumblers —copied later in coloured or pressed glass.

Vases It is impossible to cover the vast range of vases in detail; they were made in every type of glass mentioned in this book and decorated in every style.

89 TUMBLER. Jacobite example, wheel-engraved with portrait of Prince Charles Edward and '1745' (*Royal Scottish Museum*)

Unusual types include vases with covers in Bristol opaque white and possibly decorated by Edkins (1770s), and Anglo-Irish covered cut-glass vases of about the same period; 'egg-cup' vases with folded rims made in coloured glass, also of this period; and the **vase-in-hand** (more familiar in porcelain), a small vase held in a lady's hand, her cuff forming the base, in enamelled opaque white *c.* 1880s. There was a vogue among the ladies of the 1860s for trying their amateur hands at painting vases—before they retreated into POTICHOMANIA. See LUSTRE VASES.

Venetian glass The earliest Venetian pieces we have are post-1450 and very different from what we now regard as typical of Venice: massive covered goblets and vases in richly coloured glass, gilded and gemmed. What won Venice fame were the extremely thin-blown lightweight fantasies of the 16th century.

The Venetians used SODA GLASS, adding extra lime from crushed marble or sea-shells. With their rediscovery of manganese as a decolorizer (c. 1500) they claimed (rather prematurely) that their brownish-yellow or greyish glass came near to the colourlessness of natural rock crystal and called it, accordingly, *cristallo*. This could be blown very thin and, like all soda glass, cooled slowly, allowing plenty of time for the intricate fancy work in which the Venetians delighted; but it was too brittle for practical everyday use.

From the 15th century onwards they made glass in rich single colours, especially blue, green and purple, and perhaps their first milk glass (LATTIMO)—although this became more important two centuries later painted in imitation of porcelain. In this century, too, they made CALCEDONIO (*Schmelzglas*) and revived the MOSAIC and MILLEFIORI techniques. In the following century they made CRACKLE GLASS (ice glass) and the famous LATTICINIO, notably the variety called *vitro di trina* (lace glass).

The tall and elegant stemmed drinking glass (virtually a Venetian invention) had serpentine stems in the form e.g. of a dragon (fig. 90) or figure-of-eight, perhaps with double-scroll side-wings in coloured glass further embellished with pinched trailing or applied medallions representing the head of the Lion of St Mark; some stems were simply a series of hollow-blown knops. The bowls were often wide, flared and even scalloped, i.e. more for ornament than use.

90 VENETIAN GLASS. Covered goblet, dragon stem; 16th century (*Corning Glass Museum*)

This emphasis on bizarre shapes and richly coloured glass served as a substitute for engraving and enamelling, for which the thin bowls of the drinking glass were not altogether suitable. There were, nevertheless, some elaborate classical scenes enamelled in brilliant colours, made towards 1600; also delicate geometrical and dotted enamel designs on clear-glass *tazze* (shallow dishes on feet, with perhaps a rudimentary stem), on bowls for the table and on the more substantial of the goblets.

Towards 1700 the growth of FAÇON-DE-VENISE and

the demand for sturdier glassware led to a decline in the industry, followed not long after by political decline.

Verre églomisé Under-glass decoration of various kinds. The Romans placed etched gold leaf (as in ZWISCHENGOLDGLÄSER) under glass and painted it over to give a black background. There were crude 16th-century religious pictures painted directly on to glass and varnished over, and Continental and English mirrors sometimes had surrounds painted and gilded similarly.

The curious name comes from an 18th-century Frenchman, J.-B. Glomy, who framed prints with a border of black and gold painted under the glass—i.e. 'Glomy-ized'.

Walking sticks It is hard to conceive of anything less practical (or likely) than a glass walking stick, and so it may earn pride of place among FRIGGERS or NAILSEA wares. The idea seems to have originated in the days when modish women loved to dress up as Dresden shepherdesses; so they had to have a crook and it had to be chic—so why not in glass, bedecked with ribbons?

Country folk copied the idea but hung them on the wall and attached to them the same superstitions as to witch balls. Then their betters thought of putting in a screw top with sponge and smelling salts; bridegrooms were given them to ensure that they never beat their wives; fair-folk thought, more practically, of filling them with hundreds-and-thousands; and sweet-shops used them as trade-signs.

And so we find them, hollow or solid, brightly coloured externally or internally with spirals of red, blue, green and amber, some twisted into barley-sugar whirligigs (Plate 6). Early ones had a carefully ferruled end, later rounded off (and often by now broken). They are reproduced today.

Whistler, Laurence (born 1912) Outstanding English point-engraver working, except at first, on glass blown to his own design, with a steel-tipped stylus, latterly sometimes with a drill, and mixing stipple with line engraving. He also engraves window

91 WHISTLER. 'The Grass Cathedral', 1972 (*Laurence Whistler*)

panes and church windows. His work has shown three main periods: commemorative pieces with emblems; topographical—mostly pictures of houses; imaginary landscapes, often symbolic (fig. 91). Three books have been written on his work and a fourth, retrospective, was published in 1975.

Williamite glass The Whig reply to JACOBITE GLASS, issued possibly on the 50th anniversary of the Battle of the Boyne, i.e. 1740, but more probably when the Protestant Orange Order was founded (1795). They are usually wheel-engraved with a portrait of William of Orange mounted, and inscribed with a loyal toast and 'The Battle of the Boyne, 1 July 1690', the occasion when William defeated his father-in-law

James II (fig. 92). Many may have been made and/or engraved in Ireland.

Window glass In England window glass was first made by the **crown sheet** method, the soda-lime glass being blown and rotated to form a large disc that was then cut up into the required sizes; it was thin, uneven and easily broken. The **broad sheet** was introduced from Venice by Mansell *c.* 1618; this was blown glass formed into a cylinder, which was slit down the middle and heated until it opened up into a flat sheet; it was thicker, more even and smoother than crown glass, but restricted in size; it can be recognized by the slight irregularities seen e.g. on old bookcases. **Plate glass**, invented in France 1688, was not blown but cast, i.e. poured on to a metal bed, rolled flat, ground and polished; for the first time large thick smooth panes could be made.

Glass is not a solid but a supercooled fluid (whatever that may be); one corollary is that very old glass is slightly thicker at the bottom of a window, the glass having flowed downwards over the centuries. See MIRRORS; NAILSEA.

Wine-glass cooler A bowl with a notched rim, to take wine glasses resting inwards on iced water, to clean and cool them. Known also as **monteiths** (see PUNCH GLASSES), these coolers were made in the 18th century in silver, porcelain or glass. They are sometimes mistaken for punch-bowls, but the function of the notches was described in 1683 by the antiquary Anthony à Wood. Smaller versions with only two notches were for individual use, each guest being given two glasses, the used glass being put in the monteith ready for the next round but one. They are

93 WINE-GLASS COOLER. Bristol blue, possibly gilded by Isaac Jacobs (*City Art Gallery, Bristol*)

sometimes in Bristol blue (fig. 93; some signed by Jacobs), with a gilt Greek-key border (1780), or in ruby or green (1820s).

Witch balls Lustrous spheres of coloured glass so named, according to the dictionary, because they were intended to ward off witches; others think the name is corrupted from 'wish ball' (a present wishing luck) or 'watch ball'. In fact, what may be called the Nailsea-type coloured balls seem to derive from separate 17th-century sources—the silver-lustred globes that served the same purposes as a convex MIRROR and the spherical bottles of holy water once hung in the window to ward off evil.

The Nailsea types may be in flecked bottle glass, sturdy enough to be used, as they are today, as fishermen's floats; or more fragile affairs with traditional Nailsea looped decoration etc., or in plain colour. The silvered variety was made by pouring a mercury mixture inside and rotating it until the whole interior was coated. Like rolling-pins, they attracted superstitions about the need to dust them daily, breakage foretelling death in the family etc. There are plenty of modern reproductions.

Yard-of-ale The 3 (91 cm) or 4-ft (1·2 m) glass seen hanging over the bar of many a country inn is usually a trick form developed from the exaggerated version of tall (18 in; 45·7 cm) pint-size (0·6 l) FLUTE GLASS, with a foot, mentioned by Pepys (1685) as used for a toast on ceremonial occasions. In the 18th century this had a high-domed folded foot and a ball knop; in the next century a flat foot and no knop.

94 ZWISCHENGOLD-GLÄSER. Goblet decorated in colours on silver base with figures depicting the Five Senses (*Sotheby's*)

The trick glass (1825) has a hollow bulb instead of a foot. The unwary drinker finds that, as he empties it, air trapped in the bulb sprays the remainder into his face. These are still made, mainly for the pub trade.

Zwischengoldgläser A forbidding name, meaning 'gold-sandwich-glasses', for a Bohemian revival *c.* 1725 of a Roman technique. Beakers, goblets and tumblers were made with double walls which enclosed gold (sometimes silver) leaf etched with a design. The outside wall might additionally be colour-stained and engraved or enamelled. (Figs 94 and 95.)

The designs included hunting scenes, legends of saints and heraldry. There are also variations of the technique, e.g. the decoration might be painted in gold on the inner surface of the outer glass. An airtight join of the two glasses was essential to prevent deterioration.

95 ZWISCHENGOLDGLÄSER. Pair of beakers with silhouette medallions on gold and silver grounds; by J. J. Mildner, Austria, 1799; signed and dated (*Christie's*)

Appendix A

USEFUL BOOKS

General

English Glass, W. B. Honey. V & A Museum, 1946
Glass through the Ages, E. Barrington Haynes. Pelican, 1948
English Table Glass, E. M. Elville. Country Life, 1951
English Scottish and Irish Table Glass, G. B. Hughes. Batsford, 1956
English Glass, W. A. Thorpe. Black (3rd ed.) 1961
How to Identify English Glasses and Decanters, 1680–1830, D. Ash. Bell, 1962
English and Irish Antique Glass, D. C. Davis. Barker, 1965
The Pocket Book of Glass, G. Wills. Country Life, 1966
English Crystal Glass, J. Bedford. Cassell, 1966
English Glass, S. Crompton. Ward Lock, 1967
English Glass for the Collector, 1660–1860, G. B. Hughes. Lutterworth, 1967
English and Irish Glass, G. Wills. Guinness Signatures, 1968
Investing in Georgian Glass, Ward Lloyd. Crescent Press, 1969
Glass—A Guide for Beginners, G. Gros-Galliner. Muller, 1970
Early 18th-Century English Glass, Frank Davis. Hamlyn, 1971

Specialized

American glass
American Glass, G. S. & H. McKearin. Crown (N.Y.), (2nd ed.), 1950

Art glass
Tiffany Glass, M. Amaya. Studio Vista, 1967

Beilby
The Ingenious Beilbys, J. Roth. Barrie & Jenkins, 1973

Bottles
Sealed Bottles, S. Ruggles-Brise. Country Life, 1949
English Bottles and Decanters, 1650–1900, D.C. Davis. Letts, 1972

Cameos
19th-Century Cameo Glass, G. W. Beard. Ceramic Book Co., 1956

183

Commemorative
History on Glass, Arthur Churchill Ltd., 1937

Cut glass
English and Irish Cut Glass, E. M. Elville.   Country Life, 1954

Glass Pictures
The Story of Old English Glass Pictures, 1690–1810, H. G. Clarke.
     1928

Irish Glass
Irish Glass, M. S. D. Westropp.   Jenkins, 1920
Irish Glass, Phelps Warren.   Faber, 1971

Paperweights
Old Glass Paperweights, E. Bergstrom.   Faber, 1948
French Crystal Paperweights, R. Imbert and Y. Amic. Danelle
     (Paris), 1948
Antique French Paperweights, P. Jokelson. USA, 1955
Paperweights, J. Bedford.   Cassell, 1968

Sulphides
Sulphides, P. Jokelson.   Nelson, 1968

20th-century glass
Modern Glass, Ada Polak.   Faber, 1961
Modern Glass, G. W. Beard.   Studio Vista, 1968

Venetian glass
Old Venetian Glass, K. Hettes.   Spring Books, 1960.

Appendix B

MUSEUMS

Accrington, Lancs. Haworth Art Gallery (Tiffany).
Barnard Castle, Co. Durham. Bowes Museum.
Bath. American Museum in Britain, Claverton Manor.
  Holburne of Menstrie Museum.
  Museum of Art.
Bedford. Cecil Higgins Art Gallery.
Belfast. Ulster Museum.
Birmingham. City Museum and Art Gallery (19th-century,
  local).
Blackburn Museum and Art Gallery.
Bristol City Art Gallery (Bristol and Nailsea).
Burnley. Towneley Hall Art Gallery and Museum (18th-
  century).
Buxton Museum.
Cambridge. Fitzwilliam Museum.
Cardiff. National Museum of Wales.
Castleford Central Library and Museum (Victorian).
Chorley, Lancs. Astley Hall Art Gallery and Museum.
Dublin. National Museum of Ireland.
Edinburgh. Royal Scottish Museum.
Exeter. Royal Albert Memorial Museum.
Gateshead. Saltwell Park Museum.
Glyndebourne, Sussex. Glynde Place.
Hereford Museum and Art Gallery.
King's Lynn Museum and Art Gallery (drinking glasses).
London. British Museum.
  Grand Lodge Library and Museum, Freemasons Hall
    (Masonic)
  Guildhall Museum.
  Victoria and Albert Museum.
  Wallace Collection.
Maidenhead. Henry Reitlinger Bequest.
Manchester City Art Gallery.
Newcastle upon Tyne. Laing Art Gallery and Museum
    (18th-century Newcastle, Beilby, slag glass).

Norwich.   Strangers Hall, Castle Museum.
Nottingham.   Castle Museum and Art Gallery.
Nuneaton Museum and Art Gallery.
Oldham Municipal Art Gallery and Museum.
Oxford.   Ashmolean (sealed wine bottles).
Preston.   Harris Museum and Art Gallery (Victorian).
Saffron Walden Museum.
St Helens.   Pilkington Glass Museum.
South Shields Library and Museum.
Spalding Museum.
Stirling.   Smith's Institute (Scottish Glass).
Stourbridge. Brierley Hill Glass Museum, Brierley Hill
     (Stourbridge glass).
Swansea.   Glynn Vivian Art Gallery.
Wakefield City Museum.

U.S.A.

Bergstrom Art Center and Museum, Neenah, Wis. (paper-
     weights).
Corning Museum of Glass, Corning, N.Y.
Henry Francis du Pont Museum, Winterthur, Md.
Steuben Collection, N.Y.C.

ITALY

Murano, Venice.   Museo Vetrario.

INDEX